Rise of the New World Order 2: The Awakening

J. Micah'el Thomas Hays

Edited and re-released June 2016

Cover Art by David Dees

ISBN: 978-0-9889820-5-5

"Therefore humble yourselves under the mighty hand of God, that He may exalt you at the proper time, casting all your anxiety on Him, because He cares for you. Be of sober spirit, be on the alert. Your adversary, the devil, prowls around like a roaring lion, seeking someone to devour. But resist him, firm in your faith, knowing that the same experiences of suffering are being accomplished by your brethren who are in the world. After you have suffered for a little while, the God of all grace, who called you to His eternal glory in Christ, will Himself perfect, confirm, strengthen and establish you. To Him be dominion forever and ever. Amen."

*-1 Peter 5:6-11**

"Put on the full armor of God, so that you will be able to stand firm against the schemes of the devil."

*-Ephesians 6:11**

*All Bible quotes NASB unless specified otherwise

The Awakening

Preface

Greetings friend,

If you have not read my first book, ***Rise of the New World Order: The Culling of Man***, this book you are now reading will not make the best sense because it builds on and assumes you know what we went over in my first book. There is terminology and information in the first book that I reference often in this second book. Also, you need to know what my particular positions on various things are so there are no surprises for you here.

It is important for the brethren to know everything we can about Satan because he has been the leader of the New World Order since the beginning. This is a very dark and deep subject that was put upon me to sort out, and we are going to connect the dots of ancient history to formulate a focused image of who and what Satan really was and is.

If you're still with me after showing you in my first book that our holidays, including Christmas and Easter, are all Satanically-based via King Nimrod/the Antichrist, then you're a real truth-seeker and this book here will not disappoint in the least. I also told you in my first book that ***'the same group of occultists who have ruled over humanity from the beginning rule over us today'***. I will prove this to be true in the book you are reading now.

Information in this book that I'm basing my position about Satan on comes from the Bible, extra-Biblical sources such as the Book of Enoch, and the historical record of the ancient mythologies of empires gone by. I'm going to show you how the Bible confirms the reality that turned into all those ancient religions, the ones we call mythologies today.

This is probably the most revealing book ever composed about Satan, I have found none like it in existence or I wouldn't have taken the trouble to write it, just like my first book.

Have you ever wondered why God allows Satan and evil to exist in our world? Why we have to go through what we do in our everyday lives? Why doesn't God just snap His fingers and make Satan and the evil ones go away? We're going to address all this and much more.

I came across a few people since releasing my first book stating that they knew most of what was in that book, but learned a couple of new things I brought to their attention. This book you have here I would be very surprised if anyone could honestly say they knew most of it already.

With the first book I was just a concerned atheist who 'woke up' and set out to verify the New World Order conspiracy, to prove to myself and others that it was indeed real. During the course of my research I saw the light of the truth of our situation and got saved by Jesus Christ. I now pray to Him daily without fail, my life now dedicated in His service.

That first book was a lot of things to a lot of people, but to me it is the story of how I got saved by learning the truth of our situation which is contained in that first book, the first of many to come.

Therefore, make no mistake that this book is written from the point of view of a Sentinel of the Most High. I'm highly opinionated and that's all this book should be viewed as: **My exact opinion of what's going on in our world**. Everyone is entitled to their opinion; I'm just putting mine in a book after doing a ton of research and prayer.

We are sentinels educating others in His service. You are truly blessed to be brave enough to seek and acknowledge the real truth of our situation, that which is contained in my works.

"There is nothing covered up that will not be revealed, and hidden that will not be known."

-Luke 12:2

Chapter 1

HELLO AGAIN

Hey friend! It's been a couple of years since I've been able to talk to you, and all I've got to say is.......**WOW!!!**

What a ~~long, strange~~ **SPIRITUALLY ENLIGHTENING** trip it's been since releasing my first book, *'Rise of the New World Order: The Culling of Man'* at the end of January 2013. The book you are holding, my second work, ***'The Awakening'***, was released May 2015 and edited/re-released in May 2016.

I had no idea how people were going to receive my first book but it's been virtually nothing but praises from those who have taken the time to not only read that book but do their own research and genuinely come to a better understanding of what is really going on.

There is certainly a political and spiritual awakening going on in the world right now and I'm so excited to be contributing to it with these works of mine. I've also met a ton of like-minded truth-seekers through the release of my first book and subsequent spreading it all over social media. The people I am starting to band together with are all motivated and patriotic people like myself who are driven to wake up others and try to salvage our country and preserve our way of life for future generations. It's looking pretty dark right now though......

It does seem that general humanity is slowly but surely waking up and finally realizing that things in our world just aren't right, they're not getting better the way they're going and are actually getting worse, and it's largely because of the people who are perennially in power in religion, government and big business. I don't need to tell you that these people are bought-and-paid-for puppets put in place to further a specific agenda, the agenda of the Great Plan.

People are waking up to the fact that it is crystal clear that the people currently running the world don't have humanity's best interests in mind. They are supremely 'on the take' in other words, and people are finally starting to notice that all they care about is themselves. Now we know the real reason why it has **always** been like this, for thousands of years: The **Satanic** Great Plan. Satan is the god of this world and that is why it is exactly his people who get to rule the world in his stead. Until Jesus comes to take the reins of the Earth for the Millennial Kingdom we live under Satan's jurisdiction, for if it were not his to offer he wouldn't have done so to Jesus Himself as he attempted to test Him in the Gospels.

Those political-corporate puppets were put in place to ultimately do the bidding of Satan himself and people need to wake up and fast to what Satan and his followers are planning for us before it's too late. The proponents of the New World Order are looking to initiate human depopulation sooner than later and it is appearing that our time is short.

So. People are just now finally starting to wake up to the fact that the political system is intentionally screwing us over, but that is not the reason this book is named 'The Awakening' This book is called 'The Awakening' because it is meant to awaken a deeper part of your soul to the truly evil world we are born into, right into the Satanic Matrix that is thousands of years in the making and very near to conclusion of its purpose. The people running the world both in the past and today have always worshipped Satan in one form or another and this is why they were allowed to be in power to start with.

I've personally had three awakenings to do with the New World Order. The first one was that it factually existed. The second one was that it existed because it is part of God's master plan for humanity---realizing that is what converted me from an atheist to a Christian. The third one was while I was researching and writing this book, and that is that we truly live in what I would call the Satanic Matrix. Satan is the god of this world, and that is the Bible talking, not me.

These people who worship and work directly for Satan, the Illuminati, literally manufacture our reality to help create this matrix of deception and control. They control everything from the top down, with the sheeple at the bottom supporting the whole thing without even knowing it.

Now, for this book I'm going to ask you to unlearn even more of what you've been conditioned to know and believe about Christianity; pretty much all of it actually.

From my first book you now know our holidays are all based on Nimrod/the Antichrist and the Babylonian Mystery Religion, but the deception they have placed over our faith runs many layers, of which the holidays are but one.

Same deal here as the first book; I'm the researcher/writer/editor/publisher, it wouldn't happen any other way. I don't think there's a book publisher on the planet that would take on my books, so I'm still going it 'alone' except for what help I get from you and others. I really do need your help to spread the word of my books and I'll thank you now for it.

This book is being presented to build up, strengthen, and even fortify your faith by stripping off layers of deception laid down on our faith over millennia to keep you at arm's length from, and in the dark about, God. Remember, if God, Jesus, Satan and the Bible were all make-believe and manufactured by 'them' to control us, wouldn't you think the forces running the New World Order agenda would be heavily promoting the Bible as the be-all, end-all truth? Wouldn't they be promoting Christianity? No, this is not the case at all. This is because the Bible tells us exactly what is happening, and Jesus Christ is the REAL DEAL.

There is a ton of intentional disinformation and literally false prophets floating around out there covering various subjects I'm bundling together in this book. I ought to know, I had to wade through it all to get to what I finally believed to be as logical of a conclusion as possible about all of it.

In this book we will review the case that the entity Satan is real and is fully in charge and guiding the New World Order along its path to completion. It certainly does tell us this in the Bible, but we're going to make it crystal clear for those that need affirmation, clarification and realization of this seeming to be fact. It is not Buddha, Krishna or whoever the proponents of the New World Order worship. It is Satan and exactly Satan and always has been since we were put here around 6,000 years ago.

This is not the book I set out to write originally---I had no intention of writing a book about the Devil when I sat down to write my second book. It became very apparent though, and very quickly, that this was an issue that needed to be addressed immediately going forward with what is being put on me to get to you ASAP as time is ticking away.

We are at the precipice of some truly amazing and terrifying times. It is important for you to know why we are being forced to go through what is coming so you will be at peace when your physical 3D body can go on no longer, no matter the situation. Our time is short, but it might get cut much shorter so it is imperative that you wake others up to what is really going on. By showing others the truth of our situation they too may find salvation as I did by knowing the truth.

As we go forward, please remember that I'm just giving you as much pertinent information as I can, in as small of a space as I can make it. Please explore everything I'm going to talk about on your own in order to arrive at your own conclusions of truth.

Chapter 2

THE DEVIL'S IN THE DETAILS....

"We know that we are of God, and that the whole world lies in the power of the evil one."
-1 John 5:19

The Bible tells us in many verses that Satan is a real and unique entity, and that he was given power over the entire world up until the time Jesus comes back to put an end to the New World Order.

Satan is probably not who you think he is and he certainly isn't what is taught to us in the compromised 'Christian' churches. There is a lot of history about Satan that is not presented in the Bible but can be found elsewhere if you know how to connect the dots.....like we're doing in this book.

Satan is **not** God's enemy. He should virtually be looked at as God's ***employee*** who did some stuff that got him put on probation from the regular duties of his job.

Satan was originally needed in order to test us, to test our soul's interaction with the 3D world, but he stepped out of line and got in big trouble with God.

Looking at the whole picture of what's going on, it seems a divine game is being played out here on Earth. Only thing is, this game is also a test of our eternal souls.

This game tests our souls through the free will decisions of all of us under duress from Satan and his minions. God is also intervening in the meantime; trying to help us navigate along this 'Divine Plan' that He has playing out.

The proponents of the New World Order have their 'Great Plan', but that is just a cog in the works of God's Divine Plan. If you know the truth of what is happening in our world this makes logical sense. If the 'good guys' ran the show, all would be peace and love and there would be no adversity at all, no testing of our free will. For now, and for our test, the evil ones get to run the show, causing much adversity on many different facets of our reality.

As I started digging in to try and find out more about Satan/the Devil/the serpent/the dragon/etc., I invariably kept coming into contact with this character named **'Azazel'**. Azazel is a fallen angel called out in the infamous Book of Enoch. The more I dug, especially when I started looking into Azazel in particular, the more dots started being connected like in my first book with regards to King Nimrod being the human ringleader of the Great Plan, and arguably the Antichrist.

I have put together the evidence in this book to tie Azazel to both the pagan god 'Saturn', and our 'Satan' from the Bible, among other identities in many ancient mythologies he used to hide his true identity among and covertly collect worship from the humans. Azazel, Saturn and Satan are all the exact same being....with different names.

If you analyze every pagan religious system, even the first one from ancient Sumer, you will find Satan. He is always represented as one of the chief deities, and in particular whichever deity is associated with the planet **Saturn.**

Soon after Sumer fell, King Nimrod showed up ruling Babylon and then regularly appeared alongside Satan in the ancient mythologies all the way to today. Since King Nimrod is found in the second pagan religious system down from Sumer, do you know what this means? This means that every pagan religion including the Sumerian pantheon came into being ***after*** the Flood event. There are 1,500+ years of human history before Sumer that the archaeologists can't give a good accounting for, but we can. The prime source for this is the Book of Enoch and it tells of Azazel's (Satan's) exploits before the Flood, which were in fact the exact reason the Flood was needed. This is how and where 'Satan fell'.

In the Hebrew language, Satan literally means 'adversary' and is used as a proper noun in the Bible for the singular entity you will come to know as Azazel, Saturn and more.

Satan rules this planet and mankind and has since we were put here and arguably before. We are born into what I call the Saturn Matrix, which is the manufactured reality created by Satan and his minions. This is all by design in order to test our souls.

Luckily for us, there is a built-in escape hatch if you know how to open it. The escape hatch is within **you**. When you open it up; your heart, mind, body and soul, which are what you consist of, with the intention of dedicating your entire being in service to Jesus Christ, you will have effectively made your escape out of the Saturn Matrix. You just have to wait out the time in your physical body until God calls you. In the meantime, we will expend many energies to making this escape hatch known to those still trapped in the Saturn Matrix, those not yet pulled into the Boat of Salvation, those not yet counted among the saved brethren.

Chapter 2/A

SERPENT LEGEND

"And there was war in heaven, Michael and his angels waging war with the dragon. The dragon and his angels waged war, and they were not strong enough, and there was no longer a place found for them in heaven. And the great dragon was thrown down, the serpent of old who is called the devil and Satan, who deceives the whole world; he was thrown down to the earth, and his angels were thrown down with him."

-Revelation 12:7-9

The symbol of the serpent as knowledge, divinity and immortality goes back way before Moses penned the Torah, telling the story of the serpent in the Garden of Eden. The serpent-theme is a global phenomenon beginning in ancient Sumer with the pagan god 'Enki'. In fact, you're going to see that both the serpent **and** goat imagery associated with Satan started in Sumer with Enki, who was the first post-Flood representation of Satan featured in a mythology.

Enki was known as the **'lord of the Earth'**, and this coincides exactly with what the bible tells us about Satan, that he is the **'god of this world'**. Both mean the same thing. The Bible and the Sumerian myth are both telling the truth. All the mythologies that followed Sumer replicated this same exact truth over and over and over all the way to the Roman Empire 2,500 years or so later.

One of Enki's ancient symbols was what we know today as the caduceus symbol. This is today the symbol for medical/biotechnology, which is the exact path to godhood/immortality via DNA knowledge. It seems that Enki/Satan's ancient symbol was basically a visual representation of DNA.

From ancient Babylon the serpent imagery made its way to Asia, where it took on the form of a dragon. The dragon as depicted in Asia is made to look serpentine as it is based on the original serpent imagery from Sumer.

The imagery of the serpent often coincides with the occult imagery of the 'Tree of Life' from the Garden of Eden. This imagery of serpents, the Tree of Life and the sacred geometry associated with it are all ancient global phenomenon. That means that those people in North/South America, who beheld the serpent the way their European/Asian/African counterparts did, had no idea of the Biblical version of the story or what Moses wrote down about the serpent/Tree of Knowledge/Tree of Life in the Garden of Eden. The serpent symbolism had to have been originally taken and spread globally from ancient Babylon after the Flood event, right after the halting of the construction of the Tower of Babel and the splitting up by God of the languages/peoples under King Nimrod.

We're going to be immediately getting into a prickly pear of an area to nail down, and misinformation and even disinformation on this and all ancient subjects is rife. Ancient history, as I have found in my research, is open to interpretation in terms of specific dates. All of the important museums, universities, archaeological digs/property rights, everything to do with ancient history, are all under the thumb of the people running the Great Plan. They try to cover as many bases as possible to keep as much truth about the Great Plan secret but can't plug every hole in the dike. The information now freely flowing from the internet is currently circumventing their defenses.

I poured over many ancient history books that I had bought at various used book stores, supposedly about the ancient world, and there is nary a peep about the Babylonian Mystery Religion or Saturn worship. These were the Great Plan's control systems of ancient history, and there is nothing to be found in the 'history' books about it that ***they*** have put upon us. Imagine that.

There is a lot to look into about mankind's ancient history and not a lot of answers I'm finding that I feel are right. 'Their' experts can give timetables of events with ranges, sometimes BIG ranges, so people can stretch timelines to fit the agenda to keep you in the dark. I'm not talking about ancient Greece or Rome that were very well documented, but the first civilizations in Sumer/ Mesopotamia/Babylon and those immediately after.

The NWO bought-and-paid-for 'experts' give hypothesis cloaked as truth that have the potential to muddy up the waters over an agenda, maybe akin to what we have with global warming/climate change today. You know from my last book that something as simple as knowing the Sun's solar cycle is what causes the real cooling and warming of the planet shouldn't even be up for debate. You know that the minute the Sun goes down at the end of the day it gets cooler, right? Less Sun = colder, more Sun = warmer. It's not rocket science. But the United Nations-crowd has somehow managed to get thousands of 'experts on weather' to all agree that mankind is a cancer on the Earth and is causing global warming. Or climate change. Or whatever they're calling it this year. We have thousands of real experts on our side, the side of **truth,** saying it's the Sun and the solar cycle. And now it appears the Sun is heading into a cooling cycle, so you'll see them phasing out the term 'global warming' for increased use of 'climate change' to get people rattled. We know what the truth is and can see right through their Satanic one world government agenda. The same goes for ancient history and archaeology. It was co-opted by them from the get-go, especially the ancient history as that is where the truth of what is going on resides.

The best modern day archaeologists in the world today still can't tell us exactly who built the pyramids and when.....or even how they were built. How they were able to get those intricate calculations without any advanced tools. There is not a piece of heavy machinery today that could have lifted some of the gigantic stones they were working with back then. The so-called experts can't even tell us **how** they moved these gigantic stone works, let alone **who** moved them.

So let's fast-forward from the very ancient past in Sumer and the origin of serpent-symbology to the not-so-ancient past, in the time of the Greek and Roman empires BC. Satan was ***again*** symbolized as a serpent called Ouroboros, which is shown as a snake, serpent, or dragon in the shape of a circle eating its own tail. Ouroboros is basically a representation of time and its association with the cycle of life. Everything organic on the Earth is recycled over and over and over again, this being represented by a snake eating its own tail.

The Ouroboros symbol that became popular in the ancient Greek mythology appears to have originally come from Egypt, in an ancient funerary text called the ***Enigmatic Book of the Netherworld***, from the tomb of Tutankhamen circa the 14th Century BC. The gist of the text is that the god Ra (Satan) and Osiris (Nimrod/the Antichrist) are together in the underworld, united as one giant god, with two serpents holding their tails in their mouths, one coiled around the head and one coiled around the feet. In my opinion, the head is representative of Satan, the divine one from another dimension and the feet would be Satan's Earthly/3D human representative Nimrod/the Antichrist.

The term 'Ouroboros' is from the Greek, with 'ouro' meaning 'the tail' and 'boros' meaning 'eating'. The Greeks took right to this symbol and it has been widely used in ancient art and especially occult circles ever since.

Ouroboros equates to time, and the cycle of birth-life-death. These are the same attributes of the Greek god Cronus and his later Roman equivalent Saturn. Saturn is often paired directly with Ouroboros in Roman mythology imagery. They are one and the same.

Ouroboros was not only depicted as a circular image but also depicted as the symbol for infinity when the serpent was coiled in the shape of the number 8. The number 8 in the occult world is associated with the planet ***Saturn.***

The symbol of Ouroboros is also highly associated with alchemy, Hermeticism, and Gnosticism.

One other thing to bring to your attention while we're talking about ancient Greece and serpents is something called the 'Oracle at Delphi'. Before reading the following, keep in mind that Apollo is exactly King Nimrod/the Antichrist and was probably giving the people the supernatural revelations himself from his spiritual prison in the Abyss.

Nimrod's current existence would be classified as "demon" status and capable of being conjured spiritually into our dimension by the Satanists for supernatural guidance as to how to progress the Great Plan in order to break his soul out of the Abyss and into our world to take over his physically re-animated body. This could easily be what they are working on right now with the CERN/LHC project in Geneva.

Apparently, there was an area in Delphi, Greece beginning around 1,400 BC where people could go to receive supernatural revelations about many different things. It was so important that ultimately it was considered by the Greeks to be the center of the world, and it predated Greek mythology by about 600 years. When they established the Greek pantheon of Gods, Apollo was the one who became associated with the Oracle at Delphi, after he wrested it away from the giant serpent (Satan) that guarded it of course. To honor the giant serpent that Apollo defeated, Apollo's resident priestess at his temple at Delphi was called Pythia, in honor of the serpent, and this is where we get the name python today. People came from all over Greece and beyond to have their questions about the future answered by the Pythia, the resident priestess of Apollo who dwelled in the shrine.

Roman mythology virtually mirrored the Greek, and Ouroboros was identified with the god of time, Saturn, who joined the days and months of the year together like the serpent swallowing its tail.

Fast forward again to modern times, or at least within the last couple hundred years, and you have Madame Blavatsky, who you know from my first book, presenting to her followers the symbol she created for theosophy, which is the basis of the New Age religion: Ouroboros (Satan) surrounding a hexagram (star of Saturn/Satan), and a swastika (Black Sun = Saturn = Satan).

Bottom line, serpentine snake-god symbology is replete throughout global history. If Satan is really 'god of this world' as we are told in the Bible, he should show up globally in the ancient historical records. Well……he does.

Chapter 2/B

THE FALL OF MAN

"Now the serpent was more crafty than any beast of the field which the Lord God had made. And he said to the woman, 'Indeed, has God said, 'You shall not eat from any tree of the garden'?'

The woman said to the serpent, 'From the fruit of the trees of the garden we may eat; but from the fruit of the tree which is in the middle of the garden, God has said, 'You shall not eat from it or touch it, or you will die.'

The serpent said to the woman, 'You surely will not die! For God knows that in the day you eat from it your eyes will be opened, and you will be like God, knowing good and evil.'

When the woman saw that the tree was good for food, and that it was a delight to the eyes, and that the tree was desirable to make one wise, she took from its fruit and ate; and she gave also to her husband with her, and he ate. Then the eyes of both of them were opened, and they knew that they were naked; and they sewed fig leaves together and made themselves loin coverings.

They heard the sound of the Lord God walking in the garden in the cool of the day, and the man and his wife hid themselves from the presence of the Lord God among the trees of the garden.

Then the Lord God called to the man, and said to him, 'Where are you?'

He said, 'I heard the sound of You in the garden, and I was afraid because I was naked; so I hid myself.'

And He said, 'Who told you that you were naked? Have you eaten from the tree of which I commanded you not to eat?'

The man said, 'The woman whom You gave to be with me, she gave me from the tree, and I ate.' Then the Lord God said to the woman, 'What is this you have done?' And the woman said, 'The serpent deceived me, and I ate.'

The Lord God said to the serpent:

'Because you have done this,
Cursed are you more than all cattle,
And more than every beast of the field;
On your belly you will go,
And dust you will eat
All the days of your life;
And I will put enmity
Between you and the woman,
And between your seed and her seed;
He shall bruise you on the head,
And you shall bruise him on the heel."

To the woman He said,
"I will greatly multiply
Your pain in childbirth,
In pain you will bring forth children;
Yet your desire will be for your husband,
And he will rule over you.'

Then to Adam He said, 'Because you have listened to the voice of your wife, and have eaten from the tree about which

I commanded you, saying, 'You shall not eat from it'; Cursed is the ground because of you;

In toil you will eat of it all the days of your life. Both thorns and thistles it shall grow for you; And you will eat the plants of the field; -By the sweat of your face You will eat bread, till you return to the ground, because from it you were taken; for you are dust, and to dust you shall return.'

Now the man called his wife's name Eve, because she was the mother of all the living. The Lord God made garments of skin for Adam and his wife, and clothed them.

Then the Lord God said, 'Behold, the man has become like one of Us, knowing good and evil; and now, he might stretch out his hand, and take also from the tree of life, and eat, and live forever'— therefore the Lord God sent him out from the garden of Eden, to cultivate the ground from which he was taken. -

So He drove the man out; and at the east of the garden of Eden He stationed the cherubim and the flaming sword which turned every direction to guard the way to the tree of life."

-Genesis 3

Genesis 3 is the explanation of the Fall of Man, the initiation of the test of our eternal souls. There needed to be an end goal of the of the 6,000-year-long game called 'The Fall of Man', that which set in motion the Great Plan.

The ultimate goal of the game for Satan and his human minions is for mankind to achieve the knowledge (technology) to live forever in this world...to become immortal. This would, in effect, mean that Satan would be their god for eternity as the god of the 3D world.

The possibilities for mankind are virtually limitless as technology increases. The evil ones controlling the world today have ultimate power and therefore first dibs on any new technology they want. They are lining themselves up to truly be gods themselves on this planet. It is their goal to be all powerful and immortal rulers over mankind under their god, Satan, and his 3D representative the Antichrist, who is a resurrected King Nimrod.

Now let's translate briefly into what I personally believe Genesis 3 is saying, starting from the top:

Satan was smarter than any 3D being, and he knew he could mislead the newly created humans away from God, which was his job, so he did. He offered up to the first humans knowledge about the 3D world that they didn't know yet because they were new and had no experience. This included occult knowledge, and if they performed particular ceremonies in honor of Satan he would reward them with further and more intricate knowledge, even knowledge of the future.

Class began with Satan teaching the first humans about occult sex rituals. This is why it says in Genesis they felt ashamed and were compelled to cover their private parts. When God comes upon the humans not long after this, they hid from Him because they were 'naked'. God already knew what they had done and they were ashamed of their private parts because they were using them for lust-laden occult-ritual sex, as opposed to having sex for love and procreation.

Satan twisted that natural attraction that males-females have into something more than love, affection and the drive to sustain the species. He was arguably responsible for the introduction of lust into our being.

Everything in our lives revolves around sex if you think about it; it's the natural, 3D way. Our physical human bodies are still animalistic at the foundation. We have to procreate our species, all animals are driven to do so, and it all revolves around having sex. If Satan's followers could live forever on 3D Earth, they could potentially also have recreational sex forever also. This is just all the more incentive for them to do what they do. The only way they can achieve this is to harness the power of the masses of people who ***aren't*** in on the plan, the **Great Plan**.

God goes on to scold Satan in Genesis 3, with Satan represented as a serpent, telling him that He is going to put Eve's offspring at odds with Satan's offspring. ***"Satan's offspring?"*** you might be thinking? Yes, that is correct. We're going to go over this in this book how Satan was on the Earth in human form from the time mankind was put here all the way up until the time of the Flood. One only needs to read Genesis 19 to see that angels can take the form of humans, when Lot entertained the two angels of God who came to him as men. This particular verse in Genesis 3 is also telling us that Eve's offspring will win out in the end, via Jesus Christ. It is even possible that Satan had sex with Eve, and then Eve showed Adam what she was taught which caused the offense to God. We can only speculate here.

God then goes on to tell Eve that part of the consequences of her initial sexual sin will be the pain of childbirth, the result of having a lot of recreational sex. He then goes on to say that even though she will go through excruciating pain as a result of recreational sex, she will continue to desire to do it because she was now lust-filled, as all humans are after the 'fall'. This has way more to do with our 3D bodies as opposed to anything else. I think Satan has a lot of power over us in the 3D world because our divine souls are housed in the physical materials that Satan is god over: Planet Earth.

Our bodies like pleasure like no other animal and we put that at the forefront of our objectives in life, using our mighty brains to fulfill this to the maximum extent. If we can live forever, and therefore pleasure our 3D bodies forever, that is surely part of the motivation for the participants of the Great Plan.

Then in Genesis 3, God says to Adam that since he is now filled with sexual lust because of Eve, he is going to leave Adam to his own devices in Satan's world, and it's going to be a tough life. God reiterates here also that humans came out of the organic material of Earth and will return to it someday.

"By the sweat of your face You will eat bread, till you return to the ground, because from it you were taken; for you are dust, and to dust you shall return."
-Genesis 3:19

And also this just 4 verses later:

"....therefore the Lord God sent him out from the garden of Eden, to cultivate the ground from which he was taken."
-Genesis 3:23

God acknowledges that since men and women's souls were now at the mercy of our lusting for each other's physical 3D bodies, that in order to maintain some sort of civility instead of a constant state of sexual excitement seeing the opposite sex naked, He made them 'garments of skin' to cover themselves. He did this not only to cover their private parts but to cover their bodies for warmth and protection, because now they were going to have to live in Satan's cruel world as opposed to God's Heavenly Eden.

Then God goes on to pontificate to His inner circle that mankind was the highest evolved being in the 3D world, to the point that He had a soul and knew in his heart the difference between good and evil, as opposed to an animal that acts according to instinct. If mankind wished to do evil he could, including formulating the Great Plan in order to live in sexual sin forever, never having to go to Hell to pay for that sin because you're still alive in the 3D world.

Sex and the human race are so deeply intertwined it's off the chart compared to sexual relations in the rest of the animal kingdom. You throw in Satan, the other fallen angels, and the demonic spirits—all of who are sexually depraved beings—influencing our lives and our sex lives in particular, and you've got quite a minefield to navigate being a human on Earth.

God wraps up Genesis 3 by saying that if we as humans make an attempt to eat of the Tree of Life that a menacing angel will make short work of us with a 'flaming sword which turned every direction'.

Mankind is getting close to making that suicidal run at the Tree of Life, bringing Nimrod back to life in an attempt to rule forever as an immortal. Archangel Michael and the angelic army of God are prophesized in the Book of Revelation to work with Jesus and stop the Great Plan in its tracks, paving the way for the peace-and-love-ridden Millennial Kingdom.

After getting the boot out of God's good graces and the Garden of Eden, some humans went on to stay loyal to God, and some chose to follow Satan, namely the line of Cain. Some have theorized that Cain was actually the son of Satan. I have found no convincing evidence of this in particular; only that Cain's descendants were full-fledged participants in the Great Plan. I wouldn't rule it out 100% though, anything is possible in this crazy world we live in, but I think we're on the right track with what I'm laying out here.

Man's intentional fall from grace was the beginning of two reasons why we are here today. The first is represented by the most important of Jesus' Two Commandments to the brethren, which is to love, adore, appreciate, and honor God our Heavenly Father for allowing our interdimensional soul to experience what it's like to exist in a different dimension, in a 3D existence. God desires our adoration. This is what makes ***Him*** feel good, that He gets the recognition He rightly deserves. So it seems there actually is a point to every single one of our existences: It is to worship and honor God, and to also treat each other fairly because we are each a representation of God.

"And He said to him, "'You shall love the Lord your God with all your heart, and with all your soul, and with all your mind.' This is the great and foremost commandment. The second is like it, 'You shall love your neighbor as yourself.' On

these two commandments depend the whole Law and the Prophets."

-Matthew 22:37-40

The second reason we are here is to rigorously fire-test our souls. God's looking for a few good souls to return to the interdimensional world from which we came, and do bigger and better things than what they were doing before they came here.

"For the Son of Man is going to come in the glory of His Father with His angels, and will then repay every man according to his deeds."

-Matthew 16:27

I think when you die your soul comes out of the 'coma' it has been in since being downloaded into a physical body, but it will remember everything you experienced as a human being. Then we will largely all look like fools for all the stupid stuff we did while we had our chance to really prove ourselves as worthy to God.

If only the world would have dutifully followed Jesus' Two Commandments, Christianity would never have slipped into the waiting clutches of the proponents of the New World Order back in ancient Rome.

With His 'Two Commandments' Jesus is making sure to tell us to not only love God with our heart and soul, **but also through our mind.** That means to be smart about showing our respect, or ***disrespect***. By blindly following after Satan's human leaders and getting in the bad habit of never questioning them, they have deceived and twisted all things to direct worship away from God and if not towards Satan something else that is not God.

We are super-important to God, especially in the role as worshippers of Him. If you are right with God you are one of His people. The evil ones have corrupted everything between us and God if you look into it. We don't worship on the right days. By calculating the Sabbath as Saturday or Sunday we are following the Gregorian calendar, which is of man's creation, namely Satan's followers. We worship alleged images of God: the cross, Virgin Mary, paintings, statues, all kinds of idolatry which is specifically warned against, and all kinds of other blasphemy that has been foisted on naïve humans.

We're not using our ***minds*** to love God. Most people are **zombies** to God because they aren't using their **mind** to pay attention to this stuff. Our religious systems are completely corrupted and it is exactly by the Satanic ones.

Jesus says the Second Commandment is like the First. This is because we're evolved to be something that our Loving Creator envisions Himself looking like and hopefully acting like if He were to present Himself in the 3D world, which He did as Jesus Christ. They are one and the same. God manifested Himself in this world as His 'Son' Jesus. This works because God in a 3D human body as Jesus the Son is still subservient to the higher dimensional version of God, who is the Supreme Being across all dimensions. This is why Jesus prayed to God in the Gospels, but is God at the same time.

Therefore, we are literally the image of God in His eyes. We are supposed to respect each other, the mirror images of God, as we would ourselves. If you are hurting someone in this life you are also hurting yourself. You may harm them mentally or physically, but your actions harm your **soul.** We've got to respect each other and respect that human life in particular is valuable to God, and thereby should be valued by us as His representatives.

Satan's rule is to love **yourself, not your neighbor** and fully indulge **yourself** into this 3D world.

Aleister Crowley summed this up perfectly in his statement, **"Do what thou wilt shall be the whole of the Law. Love is the law, love under will."** This exactly means to do whatever you want that gives you pleasure, no matter how depraved that may be, it is your right to do it in Crowley's view, and in Satan's world. This was later morphed in the 1960s to **'If it feels good, do it'** and also **'Do your own thing'**. What it boils down to, is you're either serving yourself and your 3D Earthly desires, or you're serving Jesus and God.

God's rule is to love Him and your neighbor, in other words, ***love everyone over yourself***. It is the polar opposite of Satan's rule. It's a powerful urge, born of our 3D existence, to love one's self. To do things that bring you physical pleasure. Sex. Music. A nice meal. A videogame. Extravagant possessions. Whatever. You do all these things because they are 'fun'. They bring you physical pleasure. And what is the precise definition of 'fun'? It is exactly the satisfying of what the flesh and blood body needs or desires in order to feel good, to get those endorphins released.

The Holy Spirit is what your interdimensional soul needs in order to feel pleasure, that feeling that God is in your presence guiding your way through the trials and tribulations of life.

Through prayer, adoration and our works, we are rewarded not with physical endorphins but the presence of the Holy Spirit in our soul.

The big difference between physical pleasure and feeling the Holy Spirit is that the Holy Spirit sticks around after the physical thrill has long passed and the endorphins have exited the building, leaving your physical body empty and wanting more.

This is exactly the point of taking hardcore drugs. I've experienced many 'hard' drugs in my younger, reckless days and when you're 'high' you're on top of the world, at least in your own mind. Then you come down and are left feeling empty and all used up.

The feeling I get when I'm full of the Holy Spirit is better than any drug I've ever taken, and it never leaves me a trembling, disheveled mess. Ever. The Holy Spirit is like a dose of pure love and the only side effects are pure calm and bliss. Even knowing all the terrible things I know about our world, it never gets me down emotionally because the Holy Spirit won't let it. I'm not happy that it appears the End is near, but I'm not unhappy either. It just is what it is, all according to the Divine Plan.

If you are able to empower your faith to the point you can overcome your physical body (which I still struggle against) and choose to consistently serve God over serving yourself, then you are passing the 'test' with flying colors. If you are at the top of your class in this testing on Earth, it is my opinion that God has great things planned for you in the future after your physical body has expired. Even if you don't ace this test, as long as you're safely counted with the saved brethren you're going to be accepted into the Kingdom of God. Your ultimate placement in the afterlife, I believe, is largely based on what you did with yourself when you had the free will to do it in this world.

When you die and stand before God, with Jesus as your witness, and God asks you this very simple question, what will you say?

"Tell Me, how did you serve Me during your time on Earth? "

Chapter 2/C

SATAN IN THE BIBLE

I think it is important for you to know my interpretations of what little the Bible says about Satan.

The main reason I read and quote here from the NASB is because that was the version my mom gave me when I was 10 years old. She had it monogrammed with my name on it even, it was a big deal to her to present it to me I remember. I thought that was pretty cool to have my name on a book (!), even though I didn't have any concept like I do today of what God is. That is why I quote from the NASB in this book. If she would have given me a KJV I'd be quoting from that.

I don't purely rely on the NASB for Bible ***research and study***, however, and regularly double-check verse wordage on important Biblical verses between the NASB, KJV, The Living Bible, the 1599 Geneva Bible, the Orthodox Jewish Bible and many others for a broad spectrum of input.

In this book you're reading, I wanted to explore the most reliable source of information about our designated adversary, Satan. Obviously the best place to go to is the Bible, so we're starting there.

I'm just going to list a handful of significant verses about Satan/the Devil/the Serpent/the Dragon, all of these terms that refer to the same being, and we'll see what they tell us or at least what I believe is trying to be given to us.

When it comes to interpreting what these verses are saying, others have already given their interpretation and may be different than mine and that's fine. That's their opinion based on what they know. I'm going to give you **my** opinion based on what **I** know.

Let's also keep in mind that the Bible is meant to tell us complex things in simple terms. Don't forget the fact they didn't have typewriters or printing presses back then, and there was so much history to be crammed into a single book, those massively important events in the history of a multi-billion-year-old universe had to be kept short and sweet. Some of those complex things the Bible relays to us weren't meant to be fully understood until near the End, when 'knowledge will increase' according to the prophet Daniel, and 'people will go to and fro'. He was told to seal up the prophecy until the end when people would understand what he said.

We are exactly at that point today.

There was something else interesting that was prophesized in the Book of Daniel about the End Times:

> *"Then the king will do as he pleases, and he will exalt and magnify himself above every god and will speak monstrous things against the God of gods; and he will prosper until the indignation is finished, for that which is decreed will be done. He will show no regard for the gods of his fathers or for the desire of women, nor will he show regard for any other god; for he will magnify himself above them all. But instead he will honor a god of fortresses, a god whom his fathers did not know; he will honor him with gold, silver, costly stones and treasures. He will take action against the strongest of fortresses with the help of a foreign god; he will give great honor to those who acknowledge him and will cause them to rule over the many, and will parcel out land for a price."*
>
> *-Daniel 11:36-39*

The above quote has many specific points to take in. It says the resurrected Nimrod will project to the world that he is higher than 'every god' and 'other god(s)'. I think he will exalt and magnify himself above those gods **because he *is* many of those ancient gods in person**. He will probably take the credit as the basis of all those ancient pagan gods, especially the ones featuring the unholy trinity of the Babylonian Mystery Religion.

I have a constantly recurring thought in my mind that says that everything we are talking about in these books is going to come out in force into the mainstream world no matter what, it can't be stopped. The Satanists will be forced to admit to the truth of what is really happening and then spin it to try and get themselves off the hook before the people rally to hang them. They might even point at my books as evidence that they were just doing a job that God needed done, albeit through Satan.

The Antichrist will personally blame God for the woes of the world and get many to agree with him, that our Heavenly Father is really the evil one and Satan and the Antichrist are the good guys. This is basically their position right now anyway. They will say that God made everything including evil so if people are mad at anyone over this New World Order-business it should be at God Himself and not the people fostering the evil in order to test us.

Although there are certainly other possibilities, this could be the great deception in the End Times we are warned about. This is the excuse they use now for their organized evil to justify it to God. The people running the New World Order certainly do believe in God, and they know Jesus is the real deal for the brethren, but they willfully choose to help create the evil needed to test us. They think they have it all figured out but they really don't, falling prey to the master deceiver himself, Satan.

It says in Daniel that the Antichrist will have no desire for women. This is a given knowing how these people operate, because the Antichrist is a blasphemous, 100% agent-of-sin for Satan. The 'man of sin', right? All he desires is male-male sex, which in its original context thousands of years ago was meant to be a fixture of occult rituals to communicate with the evil entities. There were actual dedicated male temple prostitutes in Nimrod's original Babylon. This is particularly why God hates male-male sex especially; it is done in occult ceremonies to honor Satan.

This is exactly why God wiped Sodom and Gomorrah off the map. He doesn't hate the human, He hates the sinful act based purely on physical lust and not love. If the Antichrist is going to have sex at all, he wants to be tapping in to the supernatural to empower himself at every turn, and that means male-on-male sodomy performed as part of an occult/black magic ceremony to conjure the power of Satan himself. He will arguably participate in hundreds if not thousands or more Satanic ceremonies involving everything you already know those people do in those horrific ceremonies. Hundreds if not thousands of human lives will be sacrificed in his immediate presence.

It says in this prophecy of Daniel that the only 'god' that the Antichrist will honor is a 'god of fortresses' which according to other Bible translations is also taken as 'the god of power and riches' or the 'god of forces' or the 'strange god' or the 'foreign god'. Any of these could easily be attached to the persona of Satan as you will see in this book, and the verse in particular says that this god will team up with the Antichrist, who could very well be Satan's son originally.

They aren't going to be introducing any new characters in the End Times. The Antichrist is Nimrod, and the 'god of fortresses' he honors is Satan. Again, as Solomon said and this is true, there is nothing new under the Sun. I have not yet been shown who the False Prophet is, but it will probably come with time.

The rest of the verses I want to focus on do not encompass every single verse in the Bible about Satan to be sure, just the most significant in our studies here. We'll start in the order they appear in the Bible.

"When the Lord will have compassion on Jacob and again choose Israel, and settle them in their own land, then strangers will join them and attach themselves to the house of Jacob. The peoples will take them along and bring them to their place, and the house of Israel will possess them as an inheritance in the land of the Lord as male servants and female servants; and they will take their captors captive and will rule over their oppressors.

And it will be in the day when the Lord gives you rest from your pain and turmoil and harsh service in which you have been enslaved, that you will take up this taunt against the king of Babylon, and say,

"How the oppressor has ceased, And how fury has ceased!
"The Lord has broken the staff of the wicked, The scepter of rulers
Which used to strike the peoples in fury with unceasing strokes,
Which subdued the nations in anger with unrestrained persecution.
"The whole earth is at rest and is quiet; They break forth into shouts of joy.
"Even the cypress trees rejoice over you, and the cedars of Lebanon, saying,
'Since you were laid low, no tree cutter comes up against us.'
"Sheol from beneath is excited over you to meet you when you come;
It arouses for you the spirits of the dead, all the leaders of the earth;
It raises all the kings of the nations from their thrones.
"They will all respond and say to you, 'Even you have been made weak as we,
You have become like us. 'Your pomp and the music of your harps. Have been brought down to Sheol;

Maggots are spread out as your bed beneath you, And worms are your covering.'
*"How you have fallen from heaven, O star of the morning (***Lucifer in the KJV***), son of the dawn!*
You have been cut down to the earth, You who have weakened the nations!
"But you said in your heart, 'I will ascend to heaven;
I will raise my throne above the stars of God, And I will sit on the mount of assembly
In the recesses of the north. 'I will ascend above the heights of the clouds;
I will make myself like the Most High.'
"Nevertheless you will be thrust down to Sheol, To the recesses of the pit.
"Those who see you will gaze at you, They will ponder over you, saying,
'Is this the man who made the earth tremble, Who shook kingdoms,
Who made the world like a wilderness, And overthrew its cities,
Who did not allow his prisoners to go home?' "All the kings of the nations lie in glory,
Each in his own tomb.
"But you have been cast out of your tomb, Like a rejected branch,
Clothed with the slain who are pierced with a sword, Who go down to the stones of the pit
Like a trampled corpse. "You will not be united with them in burial,
Because you have ruined your country, You have slain your people.

May the offspring of evildoers not be mentioned forever. "Prepare for his sons a place of slaughter Because

of the iniquity of their fathers. They must not arise and take possession of the earth and fill the face of the world with cities."
-Isaiah 14 (The KJV uses the term 'Lucifer' in place of 'star of the morning' above)

I'm going to tell you my opinion of what this verse is talking about, and it's not Satan like most people think. Lucifer is not another name for Satan, it is another name for King Nimrod. This is particularly obvious since the beginning of the verse says it is aimed at the 'king of Babylon', who is being taunted by the Hebrews that he is in Sheol, which is the Abyss. They are taunting him because his physical body is 'dead', but his soul is active in the Abyss and can hear their taunts. Nimrod is currently the overlord of the Abyss if you'll remember:

"They have as king over them, the angel of the abyss; his name in Hebrew is Abaddon, and in the Greek he has the name Apollyon (Apollo)."
-Revelation 9:11

The term 'Lucifer' comes from Latin, and translated doesn't mean Satan, it means 'light bearer'. Satan represents the light itself, the knowledge held tight within the occult Satanic-Illuminati structure today, and Nimrod is the light/knowledge ***bearer.*** The 'Luciferians' are the proponents of the New World Order, the Illuminati, who are the bearers of the ancient occult-Satanic knowledge. The knowledge that Nimrod was given in ancient Babylon is the control system his occult followers use to rule over us today, to exploit us, and to use us as the worker bees for them to achieve godhood on Earth.

The differing terms used in the above verse in place of 'Lucifer' in other translations, such as 'day star' or 'morning star' or 'star of the morning' or 'son of the dawn', are referring to the Sun, of which Nimrod was deified in the Babylonian Mystery Religion. He was the origination of the Sun god, remember? The Sun god is the head of the BMR. The 'day star' is exactly the Sun, the only *star* you can see in the day. The 'morning star' is the Sun as it rises in the morning. The 'star of the morning' is the Sun, which is 'born' of the dawn. All of these are referring to Nimrod, the Antichrist.

2 Peter 1:19 backs up my assertion that 'day star' and 'morning star' refer to the Sun:

> *"So we have the prophetic word made more sure, to which you do well to pay attention as to a lamp shining in a dark place, until the day dawns and the ***morning star*** arises in your hearts."*
>
> *-2 Peter 1:19 NASB*

> *"We have also a more sure word of prophecy; whereunto ye do well that ye take heed, as unto a light that shineth in a dark place, until the day dawn, and the ***day star*** arise in your hearts"*
>
> *-2 Peter 1:19 KJV*

Even Jesus Himself tells us that 'morning star' means Sun:

> *"I, Jesus, have sent My angel to testify to you these things for the churches. I am the root and the descendant of David, the bright ***morning star***."*
>
> *-Revelation 22:16*

Peter here surely isn't saying that Satan himself is going to rise in your hearts, nor is he going to say Venus will arise in your heart. He's confirming that Lucifer = day star = morning star = son of the dawn = the Sun = King Nimrod as deified in the control system we live under today, the Babylonian Mystery Religion. Surely Jesus also wouldn't be equating 'morning star' with Lucifer either. Jesus didn't look at the Sun as a god, but as a good thing necessary for light and life itself.

So now that we know this verse is referring to King Nimrod, it makes a whole lot more sense.

OK. On to a tough one to pan some definitive sense out of, the infamous verse from Ezekiel. Is God talking about/to the King of Tyre or Satan? Or something different? Both? Neither? Let's read most of this verse through:

The word of the Lord came again to me, saying, "Son of man, say to the leader of Tyre,
Thus says the Lord God,
"Because your heart is lifted up
And you have said, 'I am a god,
I sit in the seat of gods
In the heart of the seas';
Yet you are a man and not God,
Although you make your heart like the heart of God—
Behold, you are wiser than Daniel;
There is no secret that is a match for you.
"By your wisdom and understanding
You have acquired riches for yourself
And have acquired gold and silver for your treasuries.
"By your great wisdom, by your trade
You have increased your riches
And your heart is lifted up because of your riches—
Therefore thus says the Lord God,
'Because you have made your heart
Like the heart of God,
Therefore, behold, I will bring strangers upon you,
The most ruthless of the nations.
And they will draw their swords
Against the beauty of your wisdom
And defile your splendor.

'They will bring you down to the pit,
And you will die the death of those who are slain
In the heart of the seas.
'Will you still say, "I am a god,"
In the presence of your slayer,
Though you are a man and not God,
In the hands of those who wound you?
'You will die the death of the uncircumcised
By the hand of strangers,
For I have spoken!' declares the Lord God!"'"
Again the word of the Lord came to me saying, "Son of man, take up a lamentation over the king of Tyre and say to him,
'Thus says the Lord God,
"You had the seal of perfection,
Full of wisdom and perfect in beauty.
"You were in Eden, the garden of God;
Every precious stone was your covering:
The ruby, the topaz and the diamond;
The beryl, the onyx and the jasper;
The lapis lazuli, the turquoise and the emerald;
And the gold, the workmanship of your settings and sockets,
Was in you.
On the day that you were created
They were prepared.
"You were the anointed cherub who covers,
And I placed you there.
You were on the holy mountain of God;
You walked in the midst of the stones of fire.
"You were blameless in your ways
From the day you were created
Until unrighteousness was found in you.
"By the abundance of your trade
You were internally filled with violence,
And you sinned;

Therefore I have cast you as profane
From the mountain of God.
And I have destroyed you, O covering cherub,
From the midst of the stones of fire.
"Your heart was lifted up because of your beauty;
You corrupted your wisdom by reason of your splendor.
I cast you to the ground;
I put you before kings,
That they may see you.
"By the multitude of your iniquities,
In the unrighteousness of your trade
You profaned your sanctuaries.
Therefore I have brought fire from the midst of you;
It has consumed you,
And I have turned you to ashes on the earth
In the eyes of all who see you.
"All who know you among the peoples
Are appalled at you;
You have become terrified
And you will cease to be forever."
-Ezekiel 28:1-19

Now, in my mind, God is clearly talking about the actual King of Tyre in the first section of the above verse and equating him exactly as following exactly in Nimrod's footsteps along the path of the Great Plan. In the first section the words of God are directed to the **'leader'** of Tyre who is a stand-in for his ***idol*** King Nimrod, but the second verse says to 'take up a lamentation ***over*** the King of Tyre', aimed at Satan's influence over the King of Tyre as Satan had influence over King Nimrod originally. The second verse I would say is directed directly at Satan.

"Then he showed me Joshua the high priest standing before the angel of the Lord, and Satan standing at his right hand to accuse him."
-Zechariah 3:1

This one is pretty self-explanatory. Satan is virtually the prosecuting attorney to God the Judge, with Jesus as our Witness, our Defense, as long as you let Him handle your case. This is further verified by the following verse:

"Then I heard a loud voice in heaven, saying,
"Now the salvation, and the power, and the kingdom of our God and the authority of His Christ have come, for the accuser of our brethren has been thrown down, he who accuses them before our God day and night."
-Revelation 12:10

What Satan is accusing us of is miserably failing our test of free will on Earth, and how good of a job ***he*** is doing to mislead us.

Now the following verse used to seriously disturb me when I was a young child, mainly because this story was in an illustrated children's book of selected Bible stories. There was an image of Satan, looking exactly like he has been imagined throughout history: Red skin, horns protruding from his head, classic Devil-goatee, hooves instead of feet, a long, red tail and a red cape to complete the ensemble. That's misleading to kids, even scary, as it was to me. That's not what Satan looks like, and all the more reason to not have any images of the Divine at all, even a representation of Satan. Imagery of any kind like that is certainly forbidden within the Ten Commandments.

"Then Jesus was led up by the Spirit into the wilderness to be tempted by the devil. And after He had fasted forty days and forty nights, He then became hungry.

And the tempter came and said to Him, "If You are the Son of God, command that these stones become bread."

But He answered and said, "It is written, 'Man shall not live on bread alone, but on every word that proceeds out of the mouth of God.'"

Then the devil took Him into the holy city and had Him stand on the pinnacle of the temple, and said to Him, "If You are the Son of God, throw Yourself down; for it is written, 'He will command His angels concerning You'; and 'On their hands they will bear You up,

So that You will not strike Your foot against a stone.'"

Jesus said to him, "On the other hand, it is written, 'You shall not put the Lord your God to the test.'"

Again, the devil took Him to a very high mountain and showed Him all the kingdoms of the world and their glory; and he said to Him, "All these things I will give You, if You fall down and worship me."

*Then Jesus *said to him, "Go, Satan! For it is written, 'You shall worship the Lord your God, and serve Him only.'"*

Then the devil left Him; and behold, angels came and began to minister to Him."

-Matthew 4:1-11

In the above verse, Jesus Himself is subject to the actions of Satan. This is because Jesus, who is the Creator God come to Earth in the flesh, was housed in a 3D physical body. Every physical thing on this planet falls under Satan's jurisdiction, even God as a physical being, Jesus Christ.

Keep in mind, as a 3D being Jesus was subjected to the same physical situation we are. He had to eat, sleep, bathe Himself, etc. He even had to work to financially support His family. Remember, He was a carpenter and made a living as a tradesman before He took up ministering full time. He would have been physically very strong to have been a carpenter in those days before power saws and forklifts like we have today. This would have made turning the tables of the moneychangers over in the temple that much easier to be certain!

His physical body was also subject to physical pain, degradation and death like we are. Even His Divine body could not withstand the sentence of torture and death by the Jews and Romans, the two factions of the Great Plan today no less, and He physically died like we all will someday. Only difference is that He came back, His physical body was brought back from the dead by the power of God. See how that works now? **Jesus beat Nimrod in the race to become the first immortal human on Earth.** In other words, God has already won the game of 'The Fall of Man' by sending Jesus into our world. It's going to continue to play out just long enough for their point-man Nimrod to come back and take the side of Satan across the finish line. Then it's game over.

So not only has God already won, but it seems Jesus went and proclaimed His victory right to the fallen angels, Nephilim and probably Nimrod in particular:

> *"For Christ also died for sins once for all, the just for the unjust, so that He might bring us to God, having been put to death in the flesh, but made alive in the spirit; in which also He went and made proclamation to the spirits now in prison, who once were disobedient, when the patience of God kept waiting in the days of Noah....."*
>
> *-1 Peter 3:18-20*

Now this following verse is one I believe gets misinterpreted by many, so I will give you my honest opinion about it:

> *"From that time Jesus began to show His disciples that He must go to Jerusalem, and suffer many things from the elders and chief priests and scribes, and be killed, and be raised up on the third day. Peter took Him aside and began to rebuke*

Him, saying, "God forbid it, Lord! This shall never happen to You." But He turned and said to Peter, "Get behind Me, Satan! You are a stumbling block to Me; for you are not setting your mind on God's interests, but man's."
-Matthew 16:21-23

This is an interesting verse. I get a strong feeling that Jesus would not have said 'Satan' as a proper noun, but 'satan' with a lowercase, indicating a noun as opposed to a pronoun. Remember, all 'satan' means in Hebrew is 'adversary'. The term 'satans' is used in the Book of Enoch to describe the Watchers, who were the fallen angels that helped Azazel/Satan corrupt all of mankind. I can't believe that Jesus would call His own disciple the 'proper name' of the 'god of this world'. He was scolding Peter for being ***adversarial*** to what He was supposed to be doing here on Earth, which was to die for our sins.

Here are two different versions of ***2 Samuel 19:22*** for comparison, the first is from the NASB and the second is from the Jewish Orthodox Bible:

*"David then said, "What have I to do with you, O sons of Zeruiah, that you should this day be an ***adversary *** to me? Should any man be put to death in Israel today? For do I not know that I am king over Israel today?"*

*"And Dovid said, "What have I to do with you, ye Bnei Tzeruyah, that ye should this day be as ***satan *** unto me? Shall there be ish put to death this day in Yisroel? For do not I know that I am this day Melech al Yisroel?"*

This following verse has been used extensively as proof that Satan has 'fallen and been kicked out of Heaven, currently residing in Hell'. This is incorrect. From the verses a couple of pages ago, it says that Satan spends night and day in Heaven accusing the brethren before God, not to mention the situation in the Book of Job where Satan is literally hanging out in Heaven with God and the other angels.

Jesus is offering up a metaphor in the context of this entire conversation here:

> *"The seventy returned with joy, saying, "Lord, even the demons are subject to us in Your name." And He said to them, "I was watching Satan fall from heaven like lightning. Behold, I have given you authority to tread on serpents and scorpions, and over all the power of the enemy, and nothing will injure you. Nevertheless do not rejoice in this, that the spirits are subject to you, but rejoice that your names are recorded in heaven."*
>
> *-Luke 10:17-20*

You've got to take into context how this conversation is going down. People have read way too much into this statement saying Satan fell from Heaven like lightning and that this is evidence he 'fell' out of God's good graces. Yes, he did do that, but Jesus is not referring to that in this verse. This is a raucous situation being described; **seventy** of Jesus' followers were whooping it up when they all met together after returning from a spiritual mission for Jesus. Imagine them all slapping each other on the back and giving each other joyous congratulations that they were winning battles over evil with Jesus backing them up. He then goes on to end the verse by saying not to become ***too*** **overjoyed** at the recent successes, as they pale in comparison to the fact that they were among the saved brethren of Jesus. What Jesus is really saying here is that Satan was, for comparable sayings, falling out of his chair that Jesus' disciples were winning out over his satanic spirits, that Satan's supernatural forces were being defeated by ***mortal*** men wielding the power of Jesus Christ.

"You heard that I said to you, 'I go away, and I will come to you.' If you loved Me, you would have rejoiced because I go to the Father, for the Father is greater than I. Now I have told you before it happens, so that when it happens, you may believe. I will not speak much more with you, for the ruler of the world is coming, and he has nothing in Me; but so that the world may know that I love the Father, I do exactly as the Father commanded Me. Get up, let us go from here."

-John 14:28-31

Clearly there is no doubt that the 'ruler of the world' that Jesus is referring to is Satan. He is confirming other verses that say the exact same thing: Satan is the god of this world, god to everyone but the saved brethren in Jesus.

"Finally, be strong in the Lord and in the strength of His might. Put on the full armor of God, so that you will be able to stand firm against the schemes of the devil. For our struggle is not against flesh and blood, but against the rulers, against the powers, against the world forces of this darkness, against the spiritual forces of wickedness in the heavenly places. Therefore, take up the full armor of God, so that you will be able to resist in the evil day, and having done everything, to stand firm. Stand firm therefore, having girded your loins with truth, and having put on the breastplate of righteousness, and having shod your feet with the preparation of the gospel of peace; in addition to all, taking up the shield of faith with which you will be able to extinguish all the flaming arrows of the evil one. And take the helmet of salvation, and the sword of the Spirit, which is the word of God."

-Ephesians 6:10-17

The apostle Paul says exactly what I believe; that we are opposed by more than just Satan. The 'rulers, powers and world forces' reside out of this world, but their influence is brought into this world by the Satanic occultists running the Great Plan.

> *"The coming of the lawless one is by the activity of Satan with all power and false signs and wonders "*
> *-2 Thessalonians 2:9*

This verse in Thessalonians tells us more than most people think. It is saying that the coming of the Antichrist, who I believe is the resurrected King Nimrod, is by the activity of Satan. What is the activity of Satan? He is actively doing two things on Earth. He is trying to lead us away from God as the supreme tester of our souls, and at the same time he is nurturing along the Great Plan, which is to attain the knowledge needed to turn man into an immortal and specifically his man, King Nimrod. So, literally by the actions of Satan guiding along the Great Plan it will result in the coming of Nimrod once again to rule over the world as he did in ancient Babylon.

I don't think this following passage needs further explanation from me:

> *"Therefore, I exhort the elders among you, as your fellow elder and witness of the sufferings of Christ, and a partaker also of the glory that is to be revealed, shepherd the flock of God among you, exercising oversight not under compulsion, but voluntarily, according to the will of God; and not for sordid gain, but with eagerness; nor yet as lording it over those allotted to your charge, but proving to be examples to the flock. And when the Chief Shepherd appears, you will receive the unfading crown of glory. You younger men, likewise, be subject to your elders; and all of you, clothe yourselves with*

humility toward one another, for God is opposed to the proud, but gives grace to the humble.

Therefore humble yourselves under the mighty hand of God, that He may exalt you at the proper time, casting all your anxiety on Him, because He cares for you. Be of sober spirit, be on the alert. Your adversary, the devil, prowls around like a roaring lion, seeking someone to devour. But resist him, firm in your faith, knowing that the same experiences of suffering are being accomplished by your brethren who are in the world. After you have suffered for a little while, the God of all grace, who called you to His eternal glory in Christ, will Himself perfect, confirm, strengthen and establish you. To Him be dominion forever and ever. Amen."

-1 Peter 5:1-11

And now, the infamous 'synagogue of Satan' verses from Revelation:

"I know your tribulation and your poverty (but you are rich), and the blasphemy by those who say they are Jews and are not, but are a synagogue of Satan."

-Revelation 2:9

"Behold, I will cause those of the synagogue of Satan, who say that they are Jews and are not, but lie—I will make them come and bow down at your feet, and make them know that I have loved you."

-Revelation 3:9

The ***'Jews who say they are Jews and are not, but lie'.*** This is so important to understand that Jesus tells us this twice, early and just as the Book of Revelation is getting underway.

The 'Jews' who were responsible for re-establishing Israel right after WWII are exactly the Synagogue of Satan Jews, the Rothschilds and their Kabbalistic cronies. They even went so far as to put the exact symbol of Satan on the Israeli flag: the hexagram. The hexagram was originally the 'star of Rephan', even before Solomon used it when he strayed from God. **'Rephan'** exactly means **'Saturn'**. Saturn (the god) is just another alias for Satan/Azazel/Cronus/Enki/etc.

Chapter 3

AZAZEL-TO HIM ASCRIBE ALL SIN

"Interpretation concerning the ages which God has made: An age to conclude [all that there is) and all that will be. Before creating them he determined [their) operations [according to the precise sequence of the ages,) one age after another age. And this is engraved on the [heavenly) tablets [for the sons of men,] (for) /[a)ll/ the ages of their dominion. This is the sequence of the son[s of Noah, from Shem to Abraham,] [unt)il he sired Isaac; the ten [generations ...] [...) Blank [...] [And] interpretation concerning 'Azalel and the angels wh(o came to rhe daughters of man] [and s]ired themselves giants. And concerning 'Azaz'el [is written ...] [to love] injustice and to let him inherit evil for all [his] ag[e . . .] [.. .] (of d1e) judgments and the judgment of the council of [...).

-Fragmentary dialogue about Azazel found in 'Ages of Creation' from the Dead Sea Scrolls, 4Q180 1:1-10.

Although there are many extra-Biblical works in existence, the two that I'm referencing here I'm only listing as they pertain to learning things about Azazel, which is an ancient alias of Satan, one of many as you're going to find.

We are leaning on the extra-Biblical works in regards to Satan in order to better get to know the one who is responsible for the New World Order, which is what my books are about.

Who knows what really happened with regards to the minimal information about Satan in the Bible. Kind of the same deal as to what happened in the pre-Flood world, the Bible just doesn't elaborate so we're going to look into everything else we can find about it all, cross-reference all the information to see what matches up, and form some sort of educated position as to what really happened in the ancient pre-Flood world, especially with regards to Satan.

Whether he was called Azazel, Enki, Cronus, Saturn, the Serpent, the Dragon, Baphomet, or today as Satan or the Devil himself, he doesn't have to hide these days. It's all coming out in the open right this second. All that 'Illuminati' hand sign stuff the rap and rock stars flash is no joke. Satan is hip, cool and **now**. When we get to ***that*** point in human civilization, and you're awake and know what's really going on, you know we're close to the end.

There is a lot of interesting information from the two extra-Biblical sources we're going to go over in this chapter, but we're going to of course go to the Bible also to see what it says about Azazel in particular. By showing that Azazel is the same entity as Saturn and Satan we get a much better picture of who Satan really is, what he does, why he does it and what he is capable of inflicting upon our world, or more accurately ***his*** world. The Bible certainly tells us more than once that Satan/Saturn/Azazel is the god of this world.

"We know that we are of God, and that the whole world lies in the power of the evil one."
-1 John 5:19

Books in this chapter, "The Book of Enoch" and "The Apocalypse of Abraham", are well known and not known to be considered blasphemous. These books will fill in many interesting details not described in the Bible and should be taken with a grain of salt, as they were not written by those considered to be prophets. That doesn't mean they weren't inspired by the Holy Spirit, however.

By cross-referencing the Bible, select extra-Biblical works, and mankind's knowledge of ancient history and religions gone-by, we are able to assemble quite a picture of Satan and everything in his sphere of influence. By knowing who he is, we are able to therefore know more about the humans working for him who are the real enemies of humanity, the modern day proponents of the Great Plan/New World Order. Remember them? The ones shoving terrorism, never-ending wars, chemtrails, 9/11, the Federal Reserve, fluoride, Agenda 21 and everything else down our throats.

The human Satanists are the real enemy of humanity, the diabolical people who sell their souls hereditarily and are perpetually running the Great Plan. They intentionally chose evil, to side with Satan against us. They feel they are filling a universal need for balance. Their evil counters the good in this world. This is their excuse, as the people running the Great Plan also believe in God. It is a devil-twisted mess for sure and the people currently running the planet have been deceived by the master deceiver himself, Satan.

> *"The 'Sons of God' have existed and do exist. From the Hindu Brahmaputras and Manasaputras (Sons of Brahma and Mind-born sons) down to the B'ne-aleim (sons of God/ Watchers) of the Jewish Bible, the faith of the centuries and universal tradition force reason to yield to such evidence....... Now the Zohar (Kabballah 'holy' book) says that the Ischin, the beautiful B'ne-aleim, were not guilty, but 'mixed themselves with mortal men because they were sent on earth to do so.' .....Their chief is Azazel. But Azazel, whom the Church dogma will associate with Satan, is nothing of the kind. Azazel is a mystery, as explained elsewhere.....There is an impenetrable mystery in the narrative concerning Azazel. And so there is, as Lanci, a librarian to the Vatican and one who ought to know, says that 'this venerable divine name has become through the pen of Biblical scholars, a devil, a wilderness, a mountain, and a he-goat'......In the Zohar, Azazel is rather the sacrificial*

victim than the 'formal adversary of Jehovah (God)' "......The amount of malicious fancy and fiction bestowed on that 'Host' (Azazel) by various fanatical writers is quite extraordinary. Azazel and his host 'are simply Hebrew 'Prometheus', and ought to be viewed from the same standpoint'

-Excerpted from Madame Helena Blavatsky's The Secret Doctrine, Vol. II, pages 374-376

Let's go now to the legendary Book of Enoch and get right into it. Azazel has the starring role........

Chapter 3/A

THE BOOK OF ENOCH

When I first started researching for the construction of my second book, I sat down and read the Book of Enoch. It's the most well-known extra-Biblical work out there, and if someone were to ever ask me if I read it I felt I would need to be able to say 'yes'. Plus, I just wanted to see what it was all about. As I was reading it I immediately had serious questions about its contents, especially this one: **Where was Satan when all this was going on before the Flood?**

There was no sign of the Satan we all knew from the Bible being responsible for leading mankind astray, only this very powerful angel named Azazel, along with another group of fallen angels called the Watchers, led by another powerful angel named Semjaza. Where was Satan?

Was he sitting on the sidelines while this was going on? And why does it say in the Book of Enoch to ***'ascribe all sin on Earth to Azazel'***? That sounds more like something Satan should be getting the credit for. It wasn't making sense. That is, until I started looking into it.

So if you haven't yet read or even heard of the 'Book of Enoch', it is the most widely known extra-Biblical work in existence today. It was considered to be of divine inspiration when it first appeared and also after, and I consider it that myself today.

Jesus Himself would have surely been aware of its existence when He was here on Earth, and the book we have today is very close to the same as it would have existed in Jesus' day. Jesus' own brother Jude quotes from the Book of Enoch in his epistle, the Book of Jude.

The Book of Enoch was arguably even considered a viable part of scripture up until the creation of the 'formal' Bible we have today at the Council of Laodicea in 364 A.D. at the hands of the Satanists themselves. This is when it was banned and then suppressed as heresy. Satan does not want you to know the details about him contained in this book, that which we are going to go over.

It is documented that the Book of Enoch was extremely popular before, during and after Jesus' ministry.... again, up until the Council of Laodicea.

Doesn't it make sense that if the Book of Enoch was propaganda by ***them*** that they would have included it in the final version of the 'Bible' they were putting together? They would ***want*** to propagate the falsehood of sinful fallen angels influencing mankind to keep the people scared and in line. But no, they wanted to hide the divine truth so they excluded it. By excluding it from the 'official' canon of scripture, it effectively was lost for roughly 1,400 years until it resurfaced around the late 1700s, slowly gaining traction from there once again.

Many of the early church elders considered it a legitimate work, including Justin Martyr, Irenaeus, Origen and Clement of Alexandria, and Tertullian. Tertullian (160-230 C.E) even went as far as calling the Book of Enoch **"Holy Scripture"**, which if there was anything blasphemous about it he certainly wouldn't have.

The first time I read the Book of Enoch it immediately did not make sense to me. I was thinking over and over, 'Where is Satan when all this is going on? There is not a mention of him in these pages" It turns out he was there the whole time. He is called Azazel in the Book of Enoch.

When reading the Book of Enoch, you've got to really pay attention to what is being said when it is talking about the fallen angels specifically. You've got to be able to see how Azazel is being specifically set apart from the other Watchers in order to give him the credentials to ID him as Satan, the god of this world, and not just the co-leader of the Watchers with Semjaza.

Also, the Book of Enoch we will be talking about is known as **1 Enoch**. There are a total of three 'Books of Enoch'. 1 Enoch is the oldest of the three, and within 1 Enoch there are 5 different sections by just as many authors, all of them unknown. What we do know is that of the part of 1 Enoch that was written the last, a section of it was quoted virtually verbatim by Jesus' own brother Jude in his epistle that is in the New Testament.

Surely Jude wouldn't quote from something Jesus would consider to be blasphemy. His acknowledgement of it in his epistle helps to validate the truth that's in it.

> *"It was also about these men that Enoch, in the seventh generation from Adam, prophesied, saying, "Behold, the Lord came with many thousands of His holy ones, to execute judgment upon all, and to convict all the ungodly of all their ungodly deeds which they have done in an ungodly way, and of all the harsh things which ungodly sinners have spoken against Him."*
>
> *-Jude 1:14-15*

> *"And behold! He comes with ten thousand Holy Ones; to execute judgment upon them and to destroy the impious, and to contend with all flesh concerning everything that the sinners and the impious have done and wrought against Him."*
>
> *-1 Enoch 1:9*

The Book of Jude was written roughly between 55 and 80 A.D. The section of 1 Enoch that contained the above quote was the newest addition to it, but still predates the Book of Jude by roughly 100 years.

1 Enoch tells us in great detail about what really happened before the Flood, why things got so bad that God had to wipe the slate clean and start over. 1 Enoch is a work of importance that I personally feel is highly significant and I certainly recommend this for your library.

Let's go to the Bible now, Book of Genesis, to review the verses that are greatly expanded on in 1 Enoch:

> *"Now it came about, when men began to multiply on the face of the land, and daughters were born to them, that the sons of God saw that the daughters of men were beautiful; and they took wives for themselves, whomever they chose.*
>
> *Then the Lord said, "My Spirit shall not strive with man forever, because he also is flesh; nevertheless his days shall be one hundred and twenty years."*
>
> *The Nephilim were on the earth in those days, and also afterward, when the sons of God came in to the daughters of men, and they bore children to them. Those were the mighty men who were of old, men of renown.*
>
> *Then the Lord saw that the wickedness of man was great on the earth, and that every intent of the thoughts of his heart was only evil continually.*
>
> *The Lord was sorry that He had made man on the earth, and He was grieved in His heart.*
>
> *The Lord said, "I will blot out man whom I have created from the face of the land, from man to animals to creeping things and to birds of the sky; for I am sorry that I have made them." But Noah found favor in the eyes of the Lord.*
>
> *These are the records of the generations of Noah. Noah was a righteous man, blameless in his time; Noah walked with God. Noah became the father of three sons: Shem, Ham, and Japheth.*
>
> *Now the earth was corrupt in the sight of God, and the earth was filled with violence. God looked on the earth, and*

behold, it was corrupt; for all flesh had corrupted their way upon the earth.

Then God said to Noah, "The end of all flesh has come before Me; for the earth is filled with violence because of them; and behold, I am about to destroy them with the earth."

-Genesis 6:1-13

When it comes to 1 Enoch, I give as much credence to it as the Bible as a source of truth. It was not God's decision to leave 1 Enoch out of the Bible, the one we hold in our hand today; it was the Unholy Roman Empire's decision. 1 Enoch should be in the Bible. It's not. Its suppression continues today and it contributes to its misinterpretation as there is a glaring hole in the story if you don't know that Azazel is really Satan.

I'm going to tell you something that you might find startling, but I believe to be the truth as it is laid out in 1 Enoch: Azazel/Satan was running the show on Earth before the Flood exactly like he does today. The only difference is, **before the Flood he was here in person, in the flesh, as a physical human-being-looking entity and he was producing offspring with human women, the most powerful of the ancient Nephilim giants.**

Azazel/Satan, the Watchers and their Nephilim offspring had a one world order going before and during the time leading right up to the Flood. The pre-Flood world is referred to as the 'Golden Age' in most mythologies, and this is exactly when 'Atlantis' was around.

The occultists are again putting the truth out in the open to hide it. Atlantis was also allegedly destroyed by a great flood. Are you seeing this now? Atlantis and the Golden Age of Man to 'them' is exactly the sinful antediluvian world to us. The Golden Age was when Azazel ruled here in the flesh, called 'Cronus' by the ancient Greeks and 'Saturn' by the Romans, among a host of other mythologies. Those mythologies are all based on the same entity, Satan.

So let's go to the very first verse in 1 Enoch and get this underway......

> *"The words of the blessing of Enoch, wherewith he blessed the elect and righteous, who will be living in the day of tribulation, when all the wicked and godless are to be removed. And he took up his parable and said: Enoch a righteous man, whose eyes were opened by God, saw the vision of the Holy One in the heavens, which the angels showed me, and from them I heard everything, and from them I understood as I saw, but not for this generation, but for a remote one which is for to come."*
>
> *-1 Enoch 1:1-2*

We today are exactly the remote generation who are approaching the days of Tribulation. I honestly believe we are right at the threshold of entering the final end game, of life as we know it coming to an abrupt end.

Today we are bearing witness the words of the prophet Daniel regarding the end times, that **'knowledge will increase'**. Not only are mankind's technological advances these days nothing short of amazing, we are being given new insight on old spiritual works; things that weren't meant to be fully understood until the time of the End. The First Book of Enoch was lost for hundreds and hundreds of years to the brethren, but reappeared just in time to fill in some of the gaps about what is going on in our world today.

1 Enoch is actually 5 different parts/books by up to 5 or even more different unknown authors. Nobody knows for sure. Various people wrote various things about Enoch and his experiences during his time on Earth---the time before the Flood.

There were probably many stories passed down about Enoch through the ancient Israelites, and the faithful ones ultimately put all of these different pieces together and called it 'The Book of Enoch'.

The 5 sections of 1 Enoch are: The Book of the Watchers, sections 1-36. The Book of Parables, sections 37-71. The Astronomical Book, sections 72-82. The Dream Visions, sections 83-90. The Epistle of Enoch, sections 91-108.

There are interjected into these 5 sections, fragments of an even more ancient book called the Book of Noah, so apparently the original writings borrowed or referenced from this particular ancient work.

Before points are marked against 1 Enoch because we don't know who wrote it, or exactly when, or even where, no one knows who wrote the Book of Job either but it's considered to be a valid part of the Old Testament.

Even in the New Testament, the Book of Hebrews remains an anonymous work but is still considered Holy writ. Is it possible that all of these sections of 1 Enoch existed in Noah's day after the Flood event but were lost to time? With only the verbal versions being passed down over the millennia?

> *"And after that my grandfather Enoch gave me the teaching of all the secrets in the book of the Parables which had been given to him, and he put them together for me in the words of the book of the Parables."*
>
> *-1 Enoch 68:1 (This is a fragment of the Book of Noah, which is contained in the section of 1 Enoch called 'The Book of Parables')*

> *"The book written by Enoch-[Enoch indeed wrote this complete doctrine of wisdom, (which is) praised of all men and a judge of all the earth] for all my children who shall dwell on the earth. And for the future generations who shall observe uprightness and peace."*
>
> *-1 Enoch 92:1*

"Another book which Enoch wrote for his son Methuselah and for those who will come after him, and keep the law in the last days. Ye who have done good shall wait for those days till an end is made of those who work evil; and an end of the might of the transgressors. And wait ye indeed till sin has passed away, for their names shall be blotted out of the book of life and out of the holy books, and their seed shall be destroyed for ever, and their spirits shall be slain, and they shall cry and make lamentation in a place that is a chaotic wilderness, and in the fire shall they burn; for there is no earth there."

-1 Enoch 108:1-3

God may have intervened in the time leading up to Jesus' arrival in order to remind people what happened in the past, and specifically before the flood involving supernatural interference, and why His coming was so important for mankind. The pages and books of 1 Enoch heralded the coming of Jesus right before He showed up in the flesh, and seem to be doing so again today.

1 Enoch speaks loudly on two highly significant issues to the brethren. First, it literally heralds the coming of Jesus in many verses, as if to pave the way for His appearance a short time later (the first time).

The second issue is that the first 1,600 years of mankind's time on Earth is truthfully barely touched on in the Bible compared to the time ***after*** the Flood. The time from Adam and Eve to the Flood event is still largely a mystery, one we're going to resolve here. A lot of very interesting stuff happened in that time, and we are told very little about it in the Bible. That detailed information was either intentionally left out to start with, or it was edited out over time, or it was intended to be known by the public just before Jesus' arrival......and His ***re*-arrival**. The gist of what we are told in the Bible is that the entire Earth became so wicked and perverted that God had to take 8 humans and start from scratch......and that's about it.

Enter 1 Enoch into the world 200-300 years before the birth of Jesus. A precise accounting of what happened before the Flood that caused the Earth to need a reset. I think the stories of what happened pre-Flood were passed down through the ages among people in general. This is exactly where the ancient mythologies got their source material, from the re-telling of the real significant events of ancient history, the biggest being the Flood.

What happened before the Flood is crucial to understanding how our world works today.

1 Enoch tells us great details about Azazel/Satan and his activities before the Flood, activities that are happening again today such as DNA experimentation and manipulation. 1 Enoch tells us exactly who the 'sons of God' were, what they did, and the true and expanded meaning of this following verse from Genesis:

> *"Now it came about, when men began to multiply on the face of the land, and daughters were born to them, that the sons of God saw that the daughters of men were beautiful; and they took wives for themselves, whomever they chose."*
> *-Genesis 6:1-2*

The 'sons of God' are angels, and in this particular verse are a group of fallen angels also known as the 'Watchers'. We are ***always*** being watched from another dimension by God, Jesus, the angels of Heaven, Azazel/Satan, and the demons/devils. They have the ability to see us, so they watch us from their dimension. Constantly. Everything we're doing. Nothing is hidden from any of these entities. But this particular group of angels, the Watchers, were lured here into our existence out of their heavenly dimension by Azazel, to take on 3D flesh bodies of their own and experience sex with beautiful human women. They did exactly this and joined Azazel in building a utopian society for their offspring the semi-divine

Nephilim, not mankind. This is the 'Golden Age wiped out by a flood' referred to in the ancient mythologies and by the occultists themselves. Mankind was delegated to subordinate status to the offspring of the 'sons of God', the Nephilim giants.

> *"The Nephilim were on the earth in those days, and also afterward, when the sons of God came in to the daughters of men, and they bore children to them. Those were the mighty men who were of old, men of renown."*
> *-Genesis 6:4*

This was not the original plan as God wanted, where Azazel was to help man along the path to godhood on Earth, the Great Plan. This all goes back to the original Divine Plan of us being tested here on Earth, with Azazel and his human followers orchestrating our test.

For your reference point, I am quoting 1 Enoch from the **R.H. Charles** translation. There are others floating around, but this is the one I ended up with a paperback copy of. There are some sections of this version that have both the Ethiopic version and the Greek as side-by-side comparisons which is nice to get two different versions to enhance the context of some verses.

In the introduction of this version by R.H.Charles, by Reverend Oesterley, he makes a particular point of the sections in 1 Enoch from the 'Book of Noah', which are fragmentary remains of what was an entire book in ancient times and which contain nearly all the references to Azazel by name in1 Enoch, and says **"These fragments are *not of much importance*; the main topics touched upon are the fall of the angels and sin among men in consequence; judgement of mankind, i.e. the Deluge, and the preservation of Noah".**

These same fragments of the Book of Noah were found among the Dead Sea Scrolls as part of 1 Enoch, and the Book of Noah is also referenced to as legitimate in the ancient Book of Jubilees, which was also found among the Dead Sea Scrolls. The Dead Sea Scrolls were written down and hidden by the Essenes, as is the most prevalent theory, so they obviously also gave merit to 1 Enoch and Jubilees also as they were important enough to them to be hidden among the Dead Sea Scrolls.

After reading and digesting the entire 1 Enoch, I can tell you without a doubt that the very sections this 'Reverend' is discrediting in the above quote are in fact the most important and telling verses in the entire book. I have a feeling that this 'Reverend' was a plant, to muddy up the water over this highly significant information. His introduction was not in the original version by R.H. Charles and I doubt Mr. Charles would have appreciated the 'Rev' downgrading this most important part of the Book of Enoch.

With regards to 1 Enoch, we're going to concentrate mainly on what it says about Azazel in particular, but also the Watchers/ fallen angels in general, and the offspring between the fallen angels and human women, which the Bible calls 'Nephilim'. The verses referring to Jesus I will address in another work.

> *"Jared lived one hundred and sixty-two years, and became the father of Enoch. Then Jared lived eight hundred years after he became the father of Enoch, and he had other sons and daughters. So all the days of Jared were nine hundred and sixty-two years, and he died.*
>
> *Enoch lived sixty-five years, and became the father of Methuselah. Then Enoch walked with God three hundred years after he became the father of Methuselah, and he had other sons and daughters. So all the days of Enoch were three hundred and sixty-five years. Enoch walked with God; and he was not, for God took him."*
>
> *-Genesis 5:18-24*

Enoch was the great-grandfather of Noah, and was an anomaly in his day. He lived to be ***only*** 365 years old, and then was taken away from Earth by God, effectively bypassing death as a human being and going directly to Heaven. He was that significant of a prophet to God. Only one other character in the Bible escaped physical death, and that was Elijah. Even Moses had to die, and I certainly don't need to bring up what happened to Jesus.

Enoch was a hugely significant personality to both God and to us today. This is why it's highly suspect that there is so little information in the Bible about not only Enoch, but what exactly happened before the Flood.

> *"By faith Enoch was taken up so that he would not see death; and he was not found because God took him up; for he obtained the witness that before his being taken up he was pleasing to God."*
>
> *-Hebrews 11:5*

What I find most intriguing about 1 Enoch, is that it clearly implicates Azazel/Satan as the primary cause of the corruption of mankind thoroughly and completely, to the point that God literally had to start over via the Flood. He had to reset. He had to wipe the slate clean with mankind and place some serious restrictions on the degree to which Azazel/Satan could influence our world as he had seriously overstepped his bounds. He was able to get around this, and was allowed to, by empowering his human representative, King Nimrod, almost immediately after the Flood.

Let's see exactly what 1 Enoch has to say about the one it says should be blamed for **all** mankind's sins: **Azazel.**

> *"....Thou seest what Azazel hath done, who hath taught all unrighteousness on earth and revealed the eternal secrets which were (preserved) in heaven, which men were striving to learn...."*
>
> *-1 Enoch 9:6 (This quote is coming from God's inner circle of angels, listed as Michael, Uriel, Raphael, and Gabriel,*

jointly addressing God as to the havoc Azazel was inflicting upon the Earth)

"And the whole earth has been corrupted through the works that were taught by Azazel: to him ascribe all sin."

-1 Enoch 10:8 (God addressing his inner circle of angels, acknowledging what they told Him in section 9 above)

"And Enoch went and said: 'Azazel, thou shalt have no peace: a severe sentence has gone forth against thee to put thee in bonds: And thou shalt not have toleration nor request granted to thee, because of the unrighteousness which thou hast taught, and because of all the works of godlessness and unrighteousness and sin which thou hast shown to men.'"

-1 Enoch 13:1-2

"And I looked and turned to another part of the earth, and saw there a deep valley with burning fire. And they brought the kings and the mighty, and began to cast them into this deep valley.

And there mine eyes saw how they made these their instruments, iron chains of immeasurable weight. And I asked the angel of peace who went with me, saying: 'For whom are these chains being prepared? '

And he said unto me: 'These are being prepared for the hosts of ***Azazel***, so that they may take them and cast them into the abyss of complete condemnation, and they shall cover their jaws with rough stones as the Lord of Spirits commanded. And Michael, and Gabriel, and Raphael, and Phanuel shall take hold of them on that great day, and cast them on that day into the burning furnace, that the Lord of Spirits may take vengeance on them for their unrighteousness in becoming subject to ***Satan*** and leading astray those who dwell on the earth.'

And in those days shall punishment come from the Lord of Spirits, and He will open all the chambers of waters which are above the heavens, and of the fountains which are beneath the earth. And all the waters shall be joined with the waters: that which is above the heavens is the masculine, and the water which is beneath the earth is the feminine. And they shall destroy all who dwell on the earth and those who dwell under the ends of the heaven. And when they have recognized their unrighteousness which they have wrought on the earth, then by these shall they perish."

-1 Enoch 54 (Note: In the above section Azazel is directly identified as 'Satan')

"And after that the Head of Days repented and said: 'In vain have I destroyed all who dwell on the earth.' And He sware by His great name: 'Henceforth I will not do so to all who dwell on the earth, and I will set a sign in the heaven: and this shall be a pledge of good faith between Me and them for ever, so long as heaven is above the earth. And this is in accordance with My command. When I have desired to take hold of them by the hand of the angels on the day of tribulation and pain because of this, I will cause My chastisement and My wrath to abide upon them,' saith God, the Lord of Spirits. 'Ye mighty kings who dwell on the earth, ye shall have to behold Mine Elect One, how He sits on the throne of glory and judges Azazel, and all his associates, and all his hosts in the name of the Lord of Spirits.'"

-1 Enoch 55 (So here it says that Azazel and his followers are to be judged by Jesus on Judgment Day)

These verses above from 1 Enoch aren't regarding some Watcher/fallen angel or even a powerful demon as most believe and would have you believe. They are exactly talking about the one we know as 'Satan'. There is no room in the antediluvian world for a 'Satan' and an 'Azazel' both being responsible for sin, they are one and the same.

1 Enoch reveals how Azazel/Satan took his job of testing mankind too far. Instead of testing us via the implementation of the Great Plan, Azazel and the Watchers started impregnating human women and created a supernatural army of Nephilim, ½ angel and ½ human to take over the planet.

Most people haven't interpreted 1 Enoch correctly and think that Azazel was just another of the fallen angels, the 'sons of God' or the 'Watchers', but we need to clarify the true context of the relationship between Azazel and Semjaza, and when you do, something becomes very clear. Semjaza is the official leader of the Watchers according to 1 Enoch and other sources, and Azazel is not depicted as subservient to Semjaza at all in 1 Enoch. In fact, Azazel is portrayed as much more the troublemaker for mankind, **extremely more** the troublemaker. This is exactly the calling card of Satan. It is Azazel and not Semjaza who gets the reverence in the Bible, and also the extra-Biblical and mythological world that we're looking into.

Azazel is credited with teaching mankind the chief pitfalls of our world today: lust for sex, materialism, and war.

Let's set the stage here at the beginning of 1Enoch, with the introduction of the fallen angels from the first chapter called 'Book of Watchers':

> *"And it came to pass when the children of men had multiplied that in those days were born unto them beautiful and comely daughters.*
>
> *And the angels, the children of the heaven, saw and lusted after them, and said to one another: 'Come, let us choose us wives from among the children of men and beget us children.'*
>
> *And Semjaza, who was their leader, said unto them: 'I fear ye will not indeed agree to do this deed, and I alone shall have to pay the penalty of a great sin.' And they all answered him and*

said: 'Let us all swear an oath, and all bind ourselves by mutual imprecations not to abandon this plan but to do this thing.'

Then sware they all together and bound themselves by mutual imprecations upon it. And they were in all two hundred; who descended in the days of Jared on the summit of Mount Hermon, and they called it Mount Hermon, because they had sworn and bound themselves by mutual imprecations upon it.

And these are the names of their leaders: Semjaza, their leader, Arakiba, Rameel, Kokabiel, Tamiel, Ramiel, Danel, Ezeqeel, Baraqijal, Asael, Armaros, Batarel, Ananel, Zaqiel, Samsapeel, Satarel, Turel, Jomjael, Sariel. These are their chiefs of tens."

-1 Enoch 6

Now, if you take note of the above mathematical numbers, it says there were 'in all two hundred' of these fallen angels. Then it goes on to list the names of the leaders of the group of 200. Counting up the list as leaders, there are 19, including Semjaza, but only the 18 under him are 'chiefs of tens'. So. 18 'chiefs of tens', plus ten lower-ranking fallen angels under their direct command, equates to 18 chiefs + 180 underling angels = 198. Add Semjaza, ***'their* leader'** , and you get 199. We're missing one to make 200 that showed up altogether on Mount Hermon. Add Azazel, who is not the leader of the Watchers, Semjaza, or an angel chief, or one of the many angels under the angel chiefs. In my opinion, Azazel had not assumed the physical form of a man up until this point. So there you have your 200 total fallen angels who came out of an otherworldly dimension into ours, and assumed physical, 3D bodies in order to have sex and procreate with human women to create the ancient race of giants called the Nephilim.

Let's keep going here with the next section of verses from 1 Enoch:

"And all the others together with them took unto themselves wives, and each chose for himself one, and they began to go in unto them and to defile themselves with them, and they taught them charms and enchantments, and the cutting of roots, and made them acquainted with plants. And they became pregnant, and they bare great giants, whose height was three thousand ells: Who consumed all the acquisitions of men. And when men could no longer sustain them, the giants turned against them and devoured mankind. And they began to sin against birds, and beasts, and reptiles, and fish, and to devour one another's flesh, and drink the blood. Then the earth laid accusation against the lawless ones."

-1 Enoch 7

This verse tells us that the fallen angels acted rebelliously and malevolently against God's directions. They showed mankind all kinds of divine knowledge we weren't supposed to know or be messing with. That is exactly what the occult is today: secret and divine knowledge that the people working for Azazel/Satan, the Illuminati, are able to harness for not only personal gain, but to further the Great Plan towards completion.

'Charms and enchantments' is black magic/spell casting. The 'cutting of roots' and making them 'acquainted with plants' has been said to mean they were taught to use them as mind-altering substances/drugs for occult ceremonies. It states that when the women became pregnant they bore the semi-divine race of the 'Nephilim', which are giant, ½ man and ½ angel offspring. These men would have been like super-men to us, super-intelligent and gigantic size giving them massive strength compared to a normal man. They were arguably the real physical and intellectual power behind building the pyramids.... overseen by their fathers, Azazel, Semjaza and the Watchers.

It says 3,000 ells in height, but that has to be a metaphor from back at the time, because 3,000 ells is about 5,000 feet---nearly a mile tall if true. This is probably an exaggeration, a figure of speech from the time 1 Enoch was written. I was not there to see these giant things alive, but I do believe that they existed and were indeed much, much larger than a normal sized man. The ancient evidence of giants on the Earth has been heavily suppressed, and even destroyed by those seeking to keep a lid on the truth, the followers of the Great Plan. There is tangible evidence those giant bones did exist in antiquity if you look into it, which I have. Giants are also depicted in ancient artwork from Babylon, Egypt, etc. The Book of Enoch tells us in great detail where they came from and what really happened with their existence here in the pre-Flood world like no other work in existence.

The next section of 1 Enoch tells us what the fallen angels were responsible for:

> *"And Azazel taught men to make swords, and knives, and shields, and breastplates, and made known to them the metals of the earth and the art of working them, and bracelets, and ornaments, and the use of antimony, and the beautifying of the eyelids, and all kinds of costly stones, and all colouring tinctures. And there arose much godlessness, and they committed fornication, and they were led astray, and became corrupt in all their ways. Semjaza taught enchantments, and root-cuttings, Armaros the resolving of enchantments, Baraqijal (taught) astrology, Kokabel the constellations, Ezeqeel the knowledge of the clouds, Araqiel the signs of the earth, Shamsiel the signs of the sun, and Sariel the course of the moon. And as men perished, they cried, and their cry went up to heaven . ."*
>
> *-1 Enoch 8*

So, within this section it tells us that it was Azazel in particular who was the most responsible for teaching mankind how to sin on many fronts.

Azazel showed mankind how to make jewelry to beautify women, and also cosmetics to further make women attractive/desirable and therefore to be lusted after even more by man and fallen angel alike.

Azazel showed man originally how to mine ore and make metals from the earth, and then turn those metals into weapons of war like swords, spears and shields for man to use against man to the death.

We are still following Azazel's game plan to this day, the Great Plan, one of the components of which is keeping mankind perpetually at war.

In the Bible, Book of Genesis, it says that ***Tubal Cain*** was responsible for discovering and bringing metals to mankind. Tubal Cain is **highly** revered by the Freemasons, and Azazel/Satan/Saturn is the god of the Freemasons. There is some odd triangle of connections going on here between Tubal Cain, Azazel and the torchbearers of the Great Plan, who today are represented by Freemasonry. There is some interesting symbolism within today's Freemasonry that revolves around Tubal Cain, represented by two balls and a cane, or sometimes a golf club, which looks like a cane. I tried to resolve this Tubal Cain-business but only have a multiple choice to offer you as of right now.

Some sources say that Azazel ***possessed*** the body of Tubal Cain and that is how Tubal Cain gained the wisdom and knowledge to be the one to introduce metallurgy to mankind. Some sources instead say that Azazel lusted after Naamah, Tubal Cain's sister. Naamah was supposedly the most beautiful woman in the world at the time, and Azazel took her for a wife and this is how Tubal Cain learned metallurgy...from his "brother-in-law" Azazel, who is Satan. There is a third option I have thought of, which I didn't find when searching, and that is that the truth about Azazel was inserted/substituted into the Bible as a metaphor through Tubal Cain. I will show you at the end of this chapter, using the Bible, how the people running the New World Order were able to partly scrub

Azazel by name out of the Old Testament. Azazel is called out by name in the Old Testament and this is a fact we will get to.

Let's go to the next section here, as this is the most important part of the entire book of 1 Enoch:

"And then Michael, Uriel, Raphael, and Gabriel looked down from heaven and saw much blood being shed upon the earth, and all lawlessness being wrought upon the earth. And they said one to another: 'The earth made without inhabitant cries the voice of their crying up to the gates of heaven. And now to you, the holy ones of heaven, the souls of men make their suit, saying, "Bring our cause before the Most High."'

And they said to the Lord of the ages: 'Lord of lords, God of gods, King of kings, and God of the ages, the throne of Thy glory (standeth) unto all the generations of the ages, and Thy name holy and glorious and blessed unto all the ages! Thou hast made all things, and power over all things hast Thou: and all things are naked and open in Thy sight, and Thou seest all things, and nothing can hide itself from Thee. Thou seest what Azazel hath done, who hath taught all unrighteousness on earth and revealed the eternal secrets which were (preserved) in heaven, which men were striving to learn: And Semjaza, to whom Thou hast given authority to bear rule over his associates.

And they have gone to the daughters of men upon the earth, and have slept with the women, and have defiled themselves, and revealed to them all kinds of sins. And the women have borne giants, and the whole earth has thereby been filled with blood and unrighteousness. And now, behold, the souls of those who have died are crying and making their suit to the gates of heaven, and their lamentations have ascended: and cannot cease because of the lawless deeds which are wrought on the earth.

And Thou knowest all things before they come to pass, and Thou seest these things and Thou dost suffer them, and Thou dost not say to us what we are to do to them in regard to these.'

-1 Enoch 9

God's good angels are around and observing us all the time. They knew that Azazel/Satan had a job to do on Earth, but he kept pushing the boundaries of his assigned duties and finally went over the limit. He did this by tempting 199 other angels to join him in the flesh on Earth. The good angels were not going to allow this to continue unchecked so they went to God to see what He wanted to do about it.

Satan is powerful, but not as powerful as God's inner circle of good angels singularly or combined, and certainly not as powerful as God Himself.

Here in verse 10 we have God's ominous response to His inner circle of angels, directing them in their duties according to His will, wielding His power:

"Then said the Most High, the Holy and Great One spake, and sent Uriel to the son of Lamech, and said to him: 'Go to Noah and tell him in My name "Hide thyself!" and reveal to him the end that is approaching: that the whole earth will be destroyed, and a deluge is about to come upon the whole earth, and will destroy all that is on it. And now instruct him that he may escape and his seed may be preserved for all the generations of the world.'

And again the Lord said to Raphael: 'Bind Azazel hand and foot, and cast him into the darkness: and make an opening in the desert, which is in Dudael, and cast him therein. And place upon him rough and jagged rocks, and cover him with darkness, and let him abide there for ever, and cover his face that he may not see light. And on the day of the great judgment he shall be cast into the fire. And heal the earth which the angels have corrupted, and proclaim the healing of the earth, that they may heal the plague, and that all the children of men may not perish through all the secret things that the Watchers have disclosed and have taught their sons. And the whole earth has been corrupted through the works that were taught by Azazel: to him ascribe all sin.'

And to Gabriel said the Lord: 'Proceed against the bastards and the reprobates, and against the children of fornication: and destroy [the children of fornication and] the children of the Watchers from amongst men [and cause them to go forth]: send them one against the other that they may destroy each other in battle: for length of days shall they not have. And no request that they (i.e. their fathers) make of thee shall be granted unto their fathers on their behalf; for they hope to live an eternal life, and that each one of them will live five hundred years.'

And the Lord said unto Michael: 'Go, bind Semjaza and his associates who have united themselves with women so as to have defiled themselves with them in all their uncleanness. And when their sons have slain one another, and they have seen the destruction of their beloved ones, bind them fast for seventy generations in the valleys of the earth, till the day of their judgment and of their consummation, till the judgment that is for ever and ever is consummated. In those days they shall be led off to the abyss of fire: and to the torment and the prison in which they shall be confined for ever. And whosoever shall be condemned and destroyed will from thenceforth be bound together with them to the end of all generations. And destroy all the spirits of the reprobate and the children of the Watchers, because they have wronged mankind. Destroy all wrong from the face of the earth and let every evil work come to an end: and let the plant of righteousness and truth appear:

and it shall prove a blessing; the works of righteousness and truth' shall be planted in truth and joy for evermore.'"
-1 Enoch 10:1-16

From everything I have taken in from 1 Enoch regarding exactly what happened to Azazel, it is my opinion that he had the privilege of having a 3D body revoked as a result of what he did with it, which was to lead the entire planet into blasphemy, including messing up the DNA of plants and animals including human beings, mixing them with unclean Nephilim blood. Azazel's physical body was destroyed but not his spiritual being. Azazel is still the 'god of this world', doing exactly what God wanted him to do to start with, which is fire test our eternal souls. He's just not around in person anymore and that was where King Nimrod and the Babylonian Mystery Religion came into being shortly after the Flood to pick up where Azazel left off.

We will take again from 1 Enoch in upcoming works of mine, but we're not done just yet with it. We need to briefly discuss the Watchers, their collective part in the corruption of the Earth, and also their part in creating the offspring that came about from angel-human mating, the 'Nephilim'.

"Now it came about, when men began to multiply on the face of the land, and daughters were born to them, that the sons of God saw that the daughters of men were beautiful; and they took wives for themselves, whomever they chose."
-Genesis 6:1

"And it came to pass when the children of men had multiplied that in those days were born unto them beautiful and comely daughters. And the angels, the children of the heaven, saw and lusted after them, and said to one another: 'Come, let us choose us wives from among the children of men and beget us children.' And Semjaza, who was their leader,

said unto them: 'I fear ye will not indeed agree to do this deed, and I alone shall have to pay the penalty of a great sin.' And they all answered him and said: 'Let us all swear an oath, and all bind ourselves by mutual imprecations not to abandon this plan but to do this thing.' Then sware they all together and bound themselves by mutual imprecations upon it. And they were in all two hundred; who descended in the days of Jared on the summit of Mount Hermon, and they called it Mount Hermon, because they had sworn and bound themselves by mutual imprecations upon it."

-1 Enoch 6:1-6

According to the quote from 1 Enoch above and the oath Semjaza required his cohorts to sign on to, it seems that the fall of the angels was a mutually-agreed-upon attempt at usurping God's eternal and ultimate authority. Azazel was arguably not part of this pact, but in my opinion it was probably Azazel who instigated this whole situation to start with, and was coming down to Earth in the flesh to rule in person whether the Watchers joined him or not.

In some circles of occult lore, Semjaza and Azazel are paired together as co-troublemakers on Earth. One version has **only the two of them** coming to Earth in the flesh and not a total of 200 angels.

At any rate, the people living on Earth at the time they showed up would have been astonished at these 'gods' that showed up who had supernatural abilities. The number and degree of their super-human abilities as angels-in-human-bodies was probably incredible, especially Azazel.

One can only imagine what life was like back then. The ancient Greeks and others referred to those days as the 'Golden Age of Man'. This is because the people running ancient Greece were full-fledged members of the Great Plan. They **APPROVED** of what Azazel and the Watchers did, giving mankind super powers of his own through DNA tampering, mixing mankind with angels.

This would be just as our scientists are working today on transhumanism and DNA tampering of all kinds in both plants and animals. You probably ate DNA-tampered food today, what is called 'GMO' food. We are back to the 'Days of Noah' it seems right this second.

> *"And they were in all two hundred; who descended in the days of Jared on the summit of Mount Hermon, and they called it Mount Hermon, because they had sworn and bound themselves by mutual imprecations upon it."*
> *-1 Enoch 6:6*

After digesting the above quote, consider this: ***The United Nations has taken the trouble to build a permanent base on Mt. Hermon, the highest altitude base of the United Nations on the planet.***

Why does the UN ***need*** a base there of all places? Because there is something very special about that particular area, and the people who control the United Nations, who are exactly the proponents of the New World Order, wanted that area secured for the time when Azazel makes his ***re***-appearance during the time of the End.

Did you ever see the movie from the 1970s called 'Close Encounters of the Third Kind' with that secret base on top of the mountain, built as a base for the aliens to land and 'enlighten' mankind?

The way that it is described in 1 Enoch it almost sounds like the fallen angels showed up in a UFO or UFOs and landed on Mt. Hermon. That's how I envision it could have gone down back in the days of Jared. When this happens again, people will think that these out-of-this-world beings are aliens from another planet that have come to save mankind. Nothing will be further from the truth at that point, and you will know who these beings are because we're going to talk about them now and all the things they did to intentionally mess up our world.

God finally had to step in and put a halt to what they had been doing and imprison them all until the time of the End. Now Satan rules by proxy, first Nimrod all the way down the ancient timeline to his followers today.

"Then He will also say to those on His left, 'Depart from Me, accursed ones, into the eternal fire which has been prepared for the devil and his angels'..."
-Matthew 25:41

"For if God did not spare angels when they sinned, but cast them into hell and committed them to chains of gloomy darkness to be kept until the judgment"
- 2 Peter 2:4

"And angels who did not keep their own domain, but abandoned their proper abode, He has kept in eternal bonds under darkness for the judgment of the great day, just as Sodom and Gomorrah and the cities around them, since they in the same way as these indulged in gross immorality and went after strange flesh, are exhibited as an example in undergoing the punishment of eternal fire."
-Jude 1:6-9

So the above quotes tell us that they have been put into interdimensional-spiritual prison so they can't physically come into our world any more. But how do we know they might be coming back to Earth?

"For the coming of the Son of Man will be just like the days of Noah. For as in those days before the flood they were eating and drinking, marrying and giving in marriage, until the day that Noah entered the ark, and they did not understand until

the flood came and took them all away; so will the coming of the Son of Man be."

-Matthew 24:37-39

"And just as it happened in the days of Noah, so it will be also in the days of the Son of Man: they were eating, they were drinking, they were marrying, they were being given in marriage, until the day that Noah entered the ark, and the flood came and destroyed them all."

-Luke 17:26

Now, the 'days of Noah' could technically be before or after the Flood. The two verses above clarify for us that Jesus is talking about the days Noah was alive ***before*** the Flood, when the Earth was populated by Azazel, fallen angels, living giants called Nephilim, and probably half-human, half-animal creatures of all kinds.

And what did the Watchers do that caused them to get into so much trouble along with Azazel?

"Then the Lord saw that the wickedness of man was great on the earth, and that every intent of the thoughts of his heart was only evil continually. The Lord was sorry that He had made man on the earth, and He was grieved in His heart. The Lord said, "I will blot out man whom I have created from the face of the land, from man to animals to creeping things and to birds of the sky; for I am sorry that I have made them."

-Genesis 6:5-7

"Then God said to Noah, "The end of all flesh has come before Me; for the earth is filled with violence because of them; and behold, I am about to destroy them with the earth."

-Genesis 6:13

"And all the others together with them took unto themselves wives, and each chose for himself one, and they began to go in unto them and to defile themselves with them, and they taught them charms and enchantments, and the cutting of roots, and made them acquainted with plants. And they became pregnant, and they bare great giants, whose height was three thousand ells: Who consumed all the acquisitions of men. And when men could no longer sustain them, the giants turned against them and devoured mankind. And they began to sin against birds, and beasts, and reptiles, and fish, and to devour one another's flesh, and drink the blood. Then the earth laid accusation against the lawless ones."
-1 Enoch 7

As if it weren't bad enough that Azazel showed mankind how to make instruments of war and how to use them, and instruct women how to accentuate their looks to enflame the lusts of men, among other things from Azazel, the Watchers also had their part in bestowing upon man forbidden knowledge.

According to 1 Enoch, the Watchers taught mankind how to make drugs and use them for occult ceremonies to make them more pliable to interacting with the interdimensional spirits. The Watchers also taught Black Magic, both how to throw a curse (hex) and how to cure/remove one:

'Semjaza taught enchantments, and root-cuttings, Armaros the resolving of enchantments.....'

1 Enoch also says the Watchers taught astrology and about the constellations. Our galaxy and universe were put together in a certain and precise way, whereby the locations of stars/constellations can tell occult knowledge. 1 Enoch also says that the Watchers taught mankind about signs/omens from the Earth and Sun. I'm not sure ***exactly*** how all of these teachings work because

I'm not an occultist, but God tells us it is not our place to know these things in many Biblical verses. This is because it represents mankind using the supernatural to attempt to eat from the Tree of Life and become immortals. The Watchers basically taught mankind how to 'cheat' to attain godhood even faster than he would have on his own.

Probably the absolute worst thing they did in God's eyes, however, was to corrupt the DNA of the life on Earth. That was the last straw. They (possibly) used Azazel's knowledge of DNA and advancing/evolving the species to try and take it even further up the evolutionary ladder than mankind, which was supposed to be the end of the evolutionary road. They did accomplish this in fact, through their children, the Nephilim. They were superior to mankind. Vastly more intelligent. Bigger. Stronger. All of it. The angels went rogue, and God eventually reined them in and destroyed all their blasphemous works.

Now, when it came time for God to lay down the 'law' through Moses, He made sure to make very clear what the most important Commandment was, placing it first:

> *"Then God spoke all these words, saying, 'I am the Lord your God, who brought you out of the land of Egypt, out of the house of slavery. You shall have no other gods before Me....' "*
>
> *-Exodus 20:1-3 This is the First and most important of the Ten Commandments. The reason for this particularly important Commandment is because other 'gods' really exist besides Azazel and seek to lead humanity astray. These are the Watchers and the spirits of their dead offspring, the Nephilim*

> *"For great is the Lord, and greatly to be praised; He also is to be feared above all gods."*
>
> *-1 Chronicles 16:25*

The whole Azazel-Watchers-Nephilim episode that caused the Flood event was a huge disrespecting to God, and He doesn't forget, and He doesn't want us to forget, so is the First Commandment regarding this.

We're going to go with a couple of quotes from the early church leaders and then close this section out; we've got a lot of information yet to get to. I'm going to save talking at length about the Nephilim for another book, as their dead spirits appear to be the 'demons' that afflict us daily. To be sure, this book is intended to be mainly about Azazel, not his demonic host.

> *"Now this posterity of Seth continued to esteem God as the Lord of the universe, and to have an entire regard to virtue, for seven generations; but in process of time they were perverted, and forsook the practices of their forefathers, and did neither pay those honors to God which were appointed to them, nor had they any concern to do justice towards men. But for what degree of zeal they had formerly shown for virtue, they now showed by their actions a double degree of wickedness; whereby they made God to be their enemy, for many angels of God accompanied with women and begat sons that proved unjust, and despisers of all that was good, on account of the confidence they had in their own strength; for the tradition is, that these men did what resembled the acts of those whom the Grecians called giants. But Noah was very uneasy at what they did; and, being displeased at their conduct, persuaded them to change their dispositions and their acts for the better; but, seeing that they did not yield to him, but were slaves to their wicked pleasures, he was afraid they would kill him, together with his wife and children, and those they had married; so he departed out of that land."*
>
> *-Flavius Josephus, from his book 'The Antiquities of the Jews', A.D. 94*

"God, when He had made the whole world, and subjected things earthly to man, and arranged the heavenly elements for the increase of fruits and rotation of the seasons, and appointed this divine law – for these things also He evidently made for man – committed the care of men and of all things under heaven to angels whom He appointed over them. But the angels transgressed this appointment, and were captivated by love of women, and begat children who are those that are called demons; and besides, they afterwards subdued the human race to themselves, partly by magical writings, and partly by fears and punishments they occasioned, and partly by teaching them to offer sacrifices, and incense, and libations, of which things they stood in need after they enslaved by lustful passions; and among men they sowed murders, wars, adulteries, intemperate needs, and all wickedness. . . ."

-Justin Martyr, from his work 'Second Apology'. He lived from 110 CE to 165 A.D.

Chapter 3/B

THE APOCALYPSE OF ABRAHAM

I came across the extra-Biblical 'Apocalypse of Abraham' after I started researching everything about Azazel in particular, and this work is truly a conviction unto itself that Azazel is Satan. Even the translators of the version I read agree with this in their footnotes talking about Azazel, named as G.H. Box, Dr. Moses Gaster, and J.I. Landsman.

It is estimated this work originated around the end of the first century or beginning of the second century A.D., no one knows for sure, and the author is unknown. It is not a prophetic work, but a latter-day expanding upon what is told to us in Genesis 15. Even though it is an anonymous work it is valid to our study of Azazel. Whoever wrote this at the time clearly knew Satan as Azazel and rightly called him out as such. It is my **opinion** that Satan was widely known as Azazel during Jesus' time, as evidenced in 1 Enoch.

This is a very short book, and there are two distinct sections contained within. The first part describes Abraham's revelation and conversion from worshipping pagan idols to worshipping the Most High God.

This leads to the second part of the book, which has to do with the Divine Revelation to Abraham that he was chosen to have a covenant with God for stepping outside the box and thinking about things for himself instead of what society had put upon him.

Abraham was able to step outside of the box and saw the light of truth. This was the ancient form of 'waking up' like you and I are right now.

God took note of Abraham's actions and called upon Abraham and his descendants to be God's beacon of light in the dark world that was completely under control of King Nimrod's Satanic Babylonian Mystery Religion at the time.

Azazel doesn't like what's unfolding in the game here in Genesis 15, and, doing what he was made to do, makes an appearance trying to ***prevent*** Abraham from teaming up with God.

Who ***but*** 'Satan' would show up to challenge God's authority over such an important scene in the Biblical verses. There is not a chance that this work is confusing Azazel with Satan. Azazel ***is*** Satan.

If this book, 'The Apocalypse of Abraham', was blasphemous it would have been called out as such a long time ago. Instead it has been buried and tamped down as 1 Enoch to try and cover Satan's tracks.

Let's first review the passage from Genesis that this book is based on:

> *"After these things the word of the Lord came to Abram in a vision, saying,*
>
> *"Do not fear, Abram,*
> *I am a shield to you;*
> *Your reward shall be very great."*
>
> *Abram said, "O Lord God, what will You give me, since I am childless, and the heir of my house is Eliezer of Damascus?"*
>
> *And Abram said, "Since You have given no offspring to me, one born in my house is my heir."*
>
> *Then behold, the word of the Lord came to him, saying, "This man will not be your heir; but one who will come forth from your own body, he shall be your heir."*

And He took him outside and said, "Now look toward the heavens, and count the stars, if you are able to count them."

And He said to him, "So shall your descendants be."

Then he believed in the Lord; and He reckoned it to him as righteousness. And He said to him, "I am the Lord who brought you out of Ur of the Chaldeans, to give you this land to possess it."

He said, "O Lord God, how may I know that I will possess it?"

So He said to him, "Bring Me a three-year-old heifer, and a three-year-old female goat, and a three-year-old ram, and a turtledove, and a young pigeon."

Then he brought all these to Him and cut them in two, and laid each half opposite the other; but he did not cut the birds. The birds of prey came down upon the carcasses, and Abram drove them away.

Now when the sun was going down, a deep sleep fell upon Abram; and behold, terror and great darkness fell upon him.

God said to Abram, "Know for certain that your descendants will be strangers in a land that is not theirs, where they will be enslaved and oppressed four hundred years. But I will also judge the nation whom they will serve, and afterward they will come out with many possessions. As for you, you shall go to your fathers in peace; you will be buried at a good old age. Then in the fourth generation they will return here, for the iniquity of the Amorite is not yet complete."

*It came about when the sun had set, that it was very dark, and behold, there appeared a smoking oven and a flaming torch which passed between these pieces. On that day the Lord made a ***covenant*** with Abram, saying,*

"To your descendants I have given this land,

From the river of Egypt as far as the great river, the river Euphrates:

The Kenite and the Kenizzite and the Kadmonite and the Hittite and the Perizzite and the Rephaim and the Amorite and the Canaanite and the Girgashite and the Jebusite."
-Genesis 15

There are 32 chapters in the 'Apocalypse of Abraham', and Azazel makes his first appearance in chapter 13 to try and prevent Abraham from going through with the sacrifice and receiving the Divine Revelation from God. I've only listed the most significant chapters from the Apocalypse of Abraham that have to do with our subject, and pay very close attention to every sentence as this book tells us many interesting things. The footnotes are also very interesting to take in when you read this book for yourself.

"And I did everything according to the commandment of the angel, and gave the angels, who had come to us, the divided animals, but the angel took the birds. And I waited for the evening sacrifice.

And there flew an unclean bird down upon the carcasses, and I drove it away. And the unclean bird spake to me, and said: "What doest thou, Abraham, upon the holy Heights, where no man eateth or drinketh, neither is there upon them (any) food of man, but these I consume everything with fire, and (will) burn thee up. Forsake the man, who is with thee, and flee; for if thou ascendest to the Heights they will make an end of thee."

And it came to pass, when I saw the bird speak, I said to the angel: "What is this, my lord?"

And he said: "This is ungodliness, this is Azazel." And he said to it: "Disgrace upon thee, Azazel! For Abraham's lot is in heaven, but thine upon the earth. Because thou hast chosen and loved this for the dwelling-(place) of thine uncleanness, therefore the eternal mighty Lord made thee a dweller upon the earth and through thee every evil spirit of lies, and through thee wrath and trials for the generations of ungodly men; for God, the Eternal, Mighty One, hath not permitted that the bodies of the righteous should be in thy hand, in order that thereby the life of the righteous and the destruction of the unclean may be assured. Hear, friend, begone with shame from me. For it hath not been given to thee to play the tempter in regard to all the righteous. Depart from this man! Thou canst not lead him astray, because he is an enemy to thee, and of those who follow thee and love what thou willest. For, behold, the vesture which in heaven was formerly thine hath been set aside for him, and the mortality which was his hath been transferred to thee."

-Apocalypse of Abraham, Chapter 13

The author of this narration is certainly calling out Azazel as Satan, even calling him the 'tempter' here in the above passage. The situation with Azazel continues into chapter 14:

"The angel said to me: "Abraham!" And I said: "Here am I, thy servant."

And he said: "Know from henceforth that the Eternal One hath chosen thee, (He) whom thou lovest; be of good courage and use this authority, so far as I bid thee, against him who slandereth truth; should I not be able to put him to shame who hath scattered over the earth the secrets of heaven and hath rebelled against the Mighty One? Say to him: 'Be thou the burning coal of the Furnace of the earth; go, Azazel, into the inaccessible parts of the earth; for thy heritage is (to be) over those existing with thee being born with the stars and clouds, with the men whose portion thou art, and (who) through thy being exist; and thine enmity is justification. On this account by thy perdition disappear from me."

And I uttered the words which the angel had taught me. And he said: "Abraham!" And I said: "Here am I, thy servant."

And the angel said to me: "Answer him not; for God hath given him power over those who do answer him."

And the angel spake to me a second time and said: "Now rather, however much he speak to thee, answer him not, that his will may have no free course in thee, because the Eternal and Mighty One hath given him weight and will; answer him not."

I did what was commanded me by the angel; and however much he spake to me, I answered him nothing whatsoever."

-Apocalypse of Abraham, Chapter 14

This verse above mirrors what we are told in 1 Enoch that Azazel **"scattered over the earth the secrets of heaven and hath rebelled against the Mighty One".**

Chapters 15 through 19 detail a spirit-vision Abraham has of visiting Heaven and other revelations, then we're back to referencing Azazel in Chapter 20:

"And the Eternal Mighty One said to me: "Abraham, Abraham!" And I said: "Here am I."

And He said: "Consider from above the stars which are beneath thee, and number, them [for Me], and make known [to Me] their number." And I said: "When can I? For I am but a man [of dust and ashes].

And He said to me: "As the number of the stars and their power, (so will) I make thy seed a nation and a people, set apart for Me in My heritage with Azazel."

And I said: "O Eternal, Mighty One! Let thy servant speak before Thee, and let not Thine anger kindle against Thy chosen one! Lo, before Thou leddest me up Azazel inveighed against me. How, then, while he is not now before Thee, hast Thou constituted Thyself with him?"

-The Apocalypse of Abraham, Chapter 20

Although it doesn't mention Azazel, we need to include chapter 21 here as a bridge to the very important chapter 22:

"And He said to me: "Look, now, beneath thy feet at the firmaments and understand the creation foreshadowed in this expanse, the creatures existing on it, and the age prepared according to it."

And I saw beneath [the surfaces of the feet, and I saw beneath] the sixth heaven and what was therein, and then the earth and its fruits, and what moved upon it and its animate beings; and the power of its men, and the ungodliness of their souls, and their righteous deeds [and the beginnings of their works], and the lower regions and the perdition therein, the Abyss and its torments. I saw there the sea and its islands, and its monsters and its fishes, and the Leviathan and his dominion, and his camping-ground, and his caves, and the world which lay upon him, and his movements, and the destructions of the world on his account.

I saw there streams and the rising of their waters, and their windings. And I saw there the Garden of Eden and its fruits, the source of the stream issuing from it, and its trees and their bloom, and those who behaved righteously. And I saw therein their foods and blessedness. And I saw there a great multitude, men and women and children, half of them on the right side of the picture and half of them on the left side of the picture."

-The Apocalypse of Abraham, Chapter 21

"And I said: "O Eternal, Mighty One! What is this picture of the creatures?"

And He said to me: "This is My will with regard to those who exist in the (divine) world-counsel, and it seemed well-pleasing before My sight, and then afterwards I gave commandment to them through My Word. And it came to pass whatever I had determined to be, was already planned beforehand in this (picture), and it stood before Me where it was created, as thou hast seen."

And I said: "O Lord, mighty and eternal! Who are the people in this picture on this side and on that?"

And He said to me: "These which are on the left side are the multitude of the peoples which have formerly been in existence and which are after thee destined, some for judgment and restoration, and others for vengeance and destruction at the end of the world. But these which are on the right side of the picture—they are the people set apart for me of the peoples with Azazel. These are they whom I have ordained to be born of thee and to be called My People."

-The Apocalypse of Abraham, Chapter 22

Here God Himself is calling out Azazel as His earthly opposition. This is Satan's job description because Satan and Azazel and the same being.

Now chapter 23:

"Now look again in the picture, who it is who seduced Eve and what is the fruit of the tree, thou wilt know what there shall be, and how it shall be to thy seed among the people at the end of the days of the age, and so far as thou canst not understand I will make known to thee, for thou art well-pleasing in my sight, and I will tell thee what is kept in my heart."

And I looked into the picture, and mine eyes ran to the side of the Garden of Eden. And I saw there a man very great in height and fearful in breadth, incomparable in aspect, embracing a woman, who likewise approximated to the aspect and shape of the man. And they were standing under a tree of (the Garden of) Eden, and the fruit of this tree was like the appearance of a bunch of grapes of the vine, and behind the tree was standing as it were a serpent in form, having hands and feet like a man's, and wings on its shoulders, six on the right side and six on the left, and they were holding the grapes of the tree in their hands, and both were eating it whom I had seen embracing.

And I said: "Who are these mutually embracing, or who is this who is between them, or what is the fruit which they are eating, O Mighty Eternal One?"

And He said: "This is the human world, this is Adam, and this is their desire upon the earth, this is Eve; but he who is between them representeth ungodliness, their beginning (on the way) to perdition, even Azazel."

And I said: "O Eternal, Mighty One! Why hast Thou given to such power to destroy the generation of men in their works upon the earth?"

And He said to me: "They who will (to do) evil—and how much I hated (it) in those who do it!—over them I gave him power, and to be beloved of them."

And I answered and said: "O Eternal, Mighty One! Wherefore hast Thou willed to effect that evil should be desired in the hearts of men, since Thou indeed art angered over that which was willed by Thee, at him who is doing what is unprofitable in thy counsel?"

-The Apocalypse of Abraham, Chapter 23

This verse calls out Azazel as Satan in the Garden of Eden. Make a special note from chapter 23 about what God says--à***"They who will (to do) evil—and how much I hated (it) in those who do it!—over them I gave him power, and to be beloved of them."***

The author of the 'Apocalypse of Abraham' is telling us here what he felt God's sentiment was towards Azazel, and how involved the true Satanists (Illuminati) are with worship of Azazel/ Satan. This is why it is exactly the highest branches of the Satanists who are the ones running the world today: Satan is the god of this world and his people run the show.

Chapter 3/C

YOM KIPPUR

If you go to Google 'images' right now, and type in 'Satan', about 90% of the images that show up are a guy in red with **horns**, a "**goat**ee", **hooves** for feet, a **tail** and interestingly enough a trident for effect. In other words, Satan is represented heavily as an entity that strongly represents a goat-like being.

The red color came about because most people believe Satan is in Hell, and that he is the ruler of Hell, so the red just goes naturally with the fires of Hell. We already know that Satan is not in Hell but travels freely between Heaven and Earth as an interdimensional being. Satan's 'trident' always is represented with **3** tines. This is the weapon that Satan wields and is arguably a representation of the unholy trinity (3 members) he founded via King Nimrod, Semiramis and Tammuz. This unholy trinity was the foundation of the Babylonian Mystery Religion, of which Satan is truly the head of.

There is no 'trinity' in my personal faith. You have God, and then you have God in human form in this dimension, which is Jesus, and that's it. The Holy Spirit is God's presence in you, that you can feel that He is right there with you. ***They*** have the trinity, **not us**. The word trinity does not exist in the Bible. It is just another deception.... like the Holidays, remember? They're all dedications to the Babylonian Mystery Religion that rules over us today.

Now, the whole point of Yom Kippur, the holiest day for the Hebrews back then and Judaism today, was to hold a ceremony to place the sins of the entire nation of Israel onto one single goat and either send it off into the wilderness/desert, or cast it off a cliff---depending on the source---and that signifies the forgiveness of sins for the nation of Israel for the previous year on that particular day, Yom Kippur. The sins were attributed to the actions of Azazel, and they were symbolically gathered up and sent back to him on a goat. The entire 'holiday' revolves around settling up with Azazel for the previous year's sins, and receiving forgiveness from God for it.

In the original Hebrew Torah, Azazel is referenced by name specifically in the Book of Leviticus. It is in the original words of the Torah that it is revealed that **the Hebrew high holiday of Yom Kippur is exactly based around Azazel, who is Satan/Saturn.**

This has since been covered up by Satan's occult followers over the millennia, replacing 'Azazel' with 'the scapegoat' in most versions of the Bible today. The modern day Orthodox Jewish Bible, the Complete Jewish Bible, the Wycliffe Bible, and the Names of God Bible are listed as the versions that still have the original name 'Azazel' in the quote:

"And Aharon shall cast lots upon the two goats; one lot for Hashem (God), and the other lot for Azazel."
-Leviticus 16:8 from the Orthodox Jewish Bible

"Then Aharon is to cast lots for the two goats, one lot for Adonai and the other for 'Az'azel."
-Leviticus 16:8 from the Complete Jewish Bible

"And Aaron shall cast lot upon ever either, one lot to the Lord, and another lot to the goat that shall be sent out. (and Aaron shall cast lots over the two goats, one lot for the Lord, and the other lot for the goat that shall be sent out, that is, the scapegoat for Azazel.)
-Leviticus 16:8 from the Wycliffe Bible

"Then Aaron must throw lots for the two goats. One lot will be for Yahweh and the other for Azazel."
-Leviticus 16:8 from the Names of God Bible

"And Aaron shall cast lots upon the two goats; one lot for the Lord, and the other lot for the scapegoat."
-Leviticus 16:8 from the King James Version

"Aaron shall cast lots for the two goats, one lot for the Lord and the other lot for the scapegoat."
-Leviticus 16:8 from the New American Standard Bible

"Then Aaron shall cast lots over the two he goats: one lot for the Lord, and the other for the Scapegoat."
-Leviticus 16:8 from the 1599 Geneva Bible

There are two other verses calling out the name of Azazel in the original Torah:

"But the goat, on which the lot fell for Azazel shall be presented chai (alive) before Hashem, to make kapporah through it, and to let him go for Azazel into the midbar."
-Leviticus 16:10, Orthodox Jewish Bible

"But the goat on which the lot for the scapegoat fell shall be presented alive before the Lord, to make atonement upon it, to send it into the wilderness as the scapegoat."
-Leviticus 16:10, New American Standard Bible

"And he that released the goat for Azazel shall immerse his garments and immerse his basar in mayim, and afterward come into the machaneh."
-Leviticus 16:26, Orthodox Jewish Bible

"The one who released the goat as the scapegoat shall wash his clothes and bathe his body with water; then afterward he shall come into the camp."
-Leviticus 16:26, New American Standard Bible

The goat imagery is also combined with the Roman name for Azazel/Satan, which is 'Saturn', and this where the mythological term 'satyr' comes from.

Satyrs are the half-goat, half-human demons/monsters described in the Bible as the 'demons of the desert'.

Here are three different translations from verse 13 Isaiah:

"But wild beasts of the desert shall lie there; and their batim (houses) shall be full of owls; and ostriches shall dwell there, and demons shall dance there."
-Isaiah 13:21, Orthodox Jewish Bible

"But wild beasts of the desert shall lie there; and their houses shall be full of doleful creatures; and owls shall dwell there, and satyrs shall dance there."
-Isaiah 13:21, King James Version

"But desert creatures will lie down there, and their houses will be full of owls;
Ostriches also will live there, and shaggy goats will frolic there."
-Isaiah 13:21, New American Standard Version

Now, to me, there is a lot of variation in the above three verses. A 'satyr' resembles closely if not exactly the god Pan from the Greek mythological pantheon. Funny thing that, because Pan is another representation of Satan. People have said that forever but you will understand exactly why.

Pan is Satan represented as a god of nature and music, and also as an animalistic sex machine, virtually the god of sex in the Greek myths. A half-goat, half-human-looking god. If you Google 'Pan the god' and search for images of him, you will basically be looking at a representation of Satan, who is Saturn, who is Azazel.

There are many quotes by various people and organizations over the years, many years in fact, agreeing with my assessment that not only is Azazel another name for Satan, but that the quotes in Leviticus should be directly attributed to him also.

Again, by showing that Azazel is the same as Kronos/Saturn, the ancient legend of the empire of Atlantis (destroyed by a flood) matches up perfectly with what we are told in 1 Enoch, how the works of Azazel (Kronos/Saturn) were destroyed by the Biblical Flood.

Chapter 4

HE WILL SEPARATE THE SHEEP FROM THE GOATS

"But when the Son of Man comes in His glory, and all the angels with Him, then He will sit on His glorious throne. All the nations will be gathered before Him; and He will separate them from one another, as the shepherd separates the sheep from the goats; and He will put the sheep on His right, and the goats on the left.

"Then the King will say to those on His right, 'Come, you who are blessed of My Father, inherit the kingdom prepared for you from the foundation of the world. For I was hungry, and you gave Me something to eat; I was thirsty, and you gave Me something to drink; I was a stranger, and you invited Me in; naked, and you clothed Me; I was sick, and you visited Me; I was in prison, and you came to Me.'

Then the righteous will answer Him, 'Lord, when did we see You hungry, and feed You, or thirsty, and give You something to drink? And when did we see You a stranger, and invite You in, or naked, and clothe You? When did we see You sick, or in prison, and come to You?'

The King will answer and say to them, 'Truly I say to you, to the extent that you did it to one of these brothers of Mine, even the least of them, you did it to Me.'

"Then He will also say to those on His left, 'Depart from Me, accursed ones, into the eternal fire which has been prepared

for the devil and his angels; for I was hungry, and you gave Me nothing to eat; I was thirsty, and you gave Me nothing to drink; I was a stranger, and you did not invite Me in; naked, and you did not clothe Me; sick, and in prison, and you did not visit Me.'

Then they themselves also will answer, 'Lord, when did we see You hungry, or thirsty, or a stranger, or naked, or sick, or in prison, and did not take care of You?'

Then He will answer them, 'Truly I say to you, to the extent that you did not do it to one of the least of these, you did not do it to Me.' These will go away into eternal punishment, but the righteous into eternal life."

-Matthew 25:31-46

Horned animals are used in general to refer to Satan, and also Nimrod, over the millennia, but it is the goat which is the dominant horned animal used to represent Satan. The unsaved sinners of the world, those of the left-hand path, those whose names were not written in the Book of Life from the beginning of time, will go to be with Satan and his demonic host in Hell at the end of time.

The saved sinners, those who have surrendered their souls to Jesus Christ and taken the 'right' path, are represented by the sheep in the above Biblical passage, for whom Jesus was the sacrificial lamb. The 'left hand path' today is synonymous with occultism/black magic/Satanism, and is also the origin of the 'left', meaning liberal politics. The one world government is a leftist-socialist-themed government. This is why professed Christians generally are almost always considered to be 'right wing' by the media and society in general.

The serpent from the Garden of Eden represents forbidden knowledge, the 'divine secrets of Heaven', as the way for mankind to achieve immortality. The goat represents mankind's animalistic 3D nature, and in particular our insatiable desire to have sex/reproduce as all animals do.

Within the human sexual world exists occult-ritual sex that can be used to communicate or even conjure demons or Satan himself to unlock the forbidden secrets of the occult and help guide the Great Plan forward towards completion. These occult sex rituals are arguably among the secrets Satan told Eve at the Garden of Eden that got them all in so much trouble, causing the shame which compelled them to cover their sexual organs in the presence of God.

The whole goat-god/horned god/stag-god theme also has to do with the simulation of the horn as an erect male reproductive organ. Horns are male-specific anyways, but serve a dual-meaning here, just like 'they' like. The term 'horny', as in desiring sex, comes exactly from this stag-god principle.

> *"...one male goat for a sin offering."*
> *-Numbers 7:16 (It goes on to repeat this exact same sentence in verses 22, 28, 34, 40, 46, 52, 58, 64, 70, 76, and 82)*

The goat is the origination of the representation of the devil/goat-horns-hand sign of heavy metal rock stars and concerts, and now virtually all musicians/rappers/politicians/the Pope/etc. It is virtually the hand sign of the left hand path. I used to hold my hands up flashing the devil horns at concerts when I was an atheist. I don't anymore; it's nothing to entertain, purely blasphemy once you're awake to the truth of it.

If I'm using my hands as a sign of paying homage to anyone these days, it's going to be clasped hands and praying to Jesus.

Chapter 4/A

BAPHOMET

From Levi's *Transcendental Magic.*

BAPHOMET, THE GOAT OF MENDES.

All the modern day imagery of Satan can ultimate be traced clear back to the image of Capricorn from at least 2,400 BC and probably earlier. The astrological sign/image of Capricorn was the first horned goat depiction of Satan, who was known as Enki, the 'Lord of the Earth' in the ancient Sumerian pantheon of gods. The Sumerian pantheon was the first mythology established after the Flood event.

Throughout the ancient mythologies, thousands of years before the particular image called Baphomet showed up, Satan was depicted as a goat-hybrid of some form or another, usually a goat-man cross, but the first image of Satan post-Flood is that of Capricorn, which was a half goat, half fish. We'll talk about Capricorn soon here, but for now we're going to focus on the figure ultimately based on Enki/Capricorn, known as Baphomet.

The earliest documented use of the term 'Baphomet' comes from around 1100 AD and culminated with the term coming out in spades at the trials of the Knights Templar, who were tried for blasphemy, homosexuality, and devil worship in the early 1300s.

The Knights Templar, as you know from my first book, rose to power due to Satan worship and were torch-bearers of the Great Plan in their day, becoming wealthy and powerful beyond anyone else at the time, including the Vatican, which is the real reason they were ultimately hunted down and exterminated. Remember, there have been at least two factions (or more) of the Great Plan in operation at any one time for millennia, only recently joining forces to pool their resources and finish the game together as a united front under Satan and the Antichrist.

The disturbing image of Baphomet is so closely associated with Satan in today's society that the official symbol of Anton LaVey's Church of Satan is the 'Sigil of Baphomet', which is the head of a goat contained within the five points of a pentagram.

> *"The symbol of Baphomet was used by the Knights Templar to represent Satan. Through the ages this symbol*

has been called by many different names. Among these are: The Goat of Mendes, The Goat of a Thousand Young, The Black Goat, The Judas Goat, and perhaps the most appropriately, The Scapegoat."

-Anton LaVey, founder of the Church of Satan, from his book, The Satanic Bible. LaVey himself says the most appropriate term for Baphomet is the term for Azazel, literally being the scapegoat for the sins of the Hebrews from the original Yom Kippur ceremony

Baphomet was also popular with Aleister Crowley:

"The Devil does not exist. It is a false name invented by the Black Brothers to imply a Unity in their ignorant muddle of dispersions. A devil who had unity would be a God... 'The Devil' is, historically, the God of any people that one personally dislikes... This serpent, SATAN, is not the enemy of Man, but He who made Gods of our race, knowing Good and Evil; He bade 'Know Thyself!' and taught Initiation. He is 'The Devil' of the Book of Thoth, and His emblem is BAPHOMET, the Androgyne who is the hieroglyph of arcane perfection... He is therefore Life, and Love. But moreover his letter is ayin, the Eye, so that he is Light; and his Zodiacal image is Capricornus, that leaping goat whose attribute is Liberty."

-Aleister Crowley, from 'Magick/Book 4'

Here, black magician/Satanist Eliphas Levi describes Baphomet:

"The goat on the frontispiece carries the sign of the pentagram on the forehead, with one point at the top, a symbol of light, his two hands forming the sign of hermetism, the one pointing up to the white moon of Chesed, the other pointing down to the black one of Geburah. This sign expresses the perfect harmony of mercy with justice. His one

arm is female, the other male like the ones of the androgyn of Khunrath, the attributes of which we had to unite with those of our goat because he is one and the same symbol. The flame of intelligence shining between his horns is the magic light of the universal balance, the image of the soul elevated above matter, as the flame, whilst being tied to matter, shines above it. The ugly beast's head expresses the horror of the sinner, whose materially acting, solely reponsible part has to bear the punishment exclusively; because the soul is insensitive according to its nature and can only suffer when it materializes. The rod standing instead of genitals symbolizes eternal life, the body covered with scales the water, the semi-circle above it the atmosphere, the feathers following above the volatile. Humanity is represented by the two breasts and the androgyn arms of this sphinx of the occult sciences."

- Eliphas Levi, from his book Dogme et Rituel de la Haute Magie ("Dogmas and Rituals of High Magic")

Levi was the artist behind the most famous image of Baphomet shown here. His words above tell us much that only the occultists have been able to understand in the past.

The 'rod standing instead of genitals' is the caduceus, and it is one of the symbols of **Enki** from the Sumerian mythology. The scales on the lower torso represent the fish part of the symbol for Capricorn, who is Enki.

Levi's image of Baphomet is also riddled with occult duality. The figure is sitting in what is called the 'as above, so below' pose. The figure has female breasts also if you'll notice, to offset the presence of the phallic caduceus placement. One white moon, one black moon. Etc.

In 2012, an Oklahoma state legislator paid out of his own pocket to have a monument to the Ten Commandments erected on state capitol land. Since this was a private and not a government-funded action, it was considered a donation to the people and the state was fine with it being on government property. After hearing about this, an organization called 'Satanic Temple' immediately began fundraising so they could pay to erect a statue of Baphomet next to the Ten Commandments monument. It's placement in Oklahoma fizzled out, so the finished statue now sits in Detroit, Michigan as of July 2015.

The Satanists are coming out into the open now, as they are increasingly accepted into our ever-liberal (left-hand path) world.

Chapter 4/B

PAN

"Pan was a composite creature, the upper part–with the exception of his horns–being human, and the lower part in the form of a goat. (...) The pipes of Pan signify the natural harmony of the spheres, and the god himself is a symbol of Saturn because this planet is enthroned in Capricorn, whose emblem is a goat"

-Freemasonic 'prophet' and confirmed 33rd degree Freemason Manly P. Hall, from his book 'Secret Teachings of All Ages'

The Greek god 'Pan' is quite an interesting character. He was the 'rock star' of the Greek pantheon of gods, playing his syrinx all day and indulging himself with his 'groupies', beautiful supernatural forest maidens called nymphs.

The Satanic Bible lists the god Pan as one of the 'Infernal Names of Satan', along with many others that are indeed correct including **Azazel.** Satan is the god of a thousand names......just like King Nimrod, and it is that way intentionally. The same 2 original and real characters passed down the millennia with different names but retaining the same symbols and attributes in order to specifically direct worship and adoration to them and away from God.

The most famous image of illustrious Satanist and 33rd degree Freemason Aleister Crowley is him wearing his pyramid hat with the all-seeing eye on the front, giving what is called the 'sign of

Pan', with his thumbs extended to simulate the horns. Crowley also wrote poetry about Pan that is quite interesting, just more for you to look into.

Pan was just another representation of Satan in his classic goat imagery, and appeared in the ancient Greek mythology sometime around 800-700 BC. He was based on the original goat-imagery of Satan as Capricorn from ancient Sumer that was passed down the line as it was in the Bible.

Pan means 'all' in Greek, and he was called Pan because **all** of the worship to **all** the Greek gods ultimately pays homage to the one that Pan represents, who is Satan, the ultimate deceiver of mankind. This is where the term '**pan**theon' comes from. The pantheon of the gods means literally 'all the gods'.

Pan was known as the god of many different things, including nature, Spring time, shepherds and their flocks, music, and fertility/sexuality among others. He is also credited with teaching prophecy to ***Apollo*** in particular, who you know as another incarnation of the original Sun god, King Nimrod.

In the classic Greek story of Pan, he was associated with the constellation of Capricorn (again, no surprise), who during an epic battle between the Titan Typhon and the Olympians jumped into a river in terror to avoid the fighting and changed into the form of Capricorn, with his bottom half turning into a fish and the upper part turning into a goat-human. This is a direct reference that Pan and Capricorn are one and the same. This story is the origination of the terms '**pan**ic' and '**pan**demonium', which means a sudden fright that comes over someone or a group of people.

> *"The true name of Satan, the Kabalists say, is that of Yahveh reversed; for Satan is not a black god, but the negation of God. The Devil is the personification of Atheism or Idolatry.*
>
> *For the Initiates, this is not a Person, but a Force, created for good, but which may serve for evil. It is the instrument of Liberty or Free Will. They represent this Force, which presides over the physical generation, under the mythologic and horned form of the God PAN; thence came the he-goat of the Sabbat, brother of the Ancient Serpent, and the Light-bearer or Phosphor, of which the poets have made the false Lucifer of the legend."*
>
> *-Albert Pike, confirmed 33rd Degree Freemasonic 'prophet' from his book "Morals and Dogma"*

The story of **Pan**dora in classical Greek mythology relates virtually like the story of the Garden of Eden, with the Torah penned by Moses over 500 years prior. Pandora was the first woman on Earth, created by Hephaestus (another version of Satan) as ordered by Zeus (another version of Nimrod). Hephaestus created Pandora using water and earth.

When Prometheus (yet another version of Satan) stole fire (knowledge/secrets) from heaven and gave it to mankind, Zeus took his revenge by giving Pandora to Prometheus' brother Epimetheus (who plays the role of Adam). Pandora was given a wedding gift of a jar, called famously Pandora's Box, with explicit directions to not open it under any circumstance. Her curiosity got the better of her and she opened it. All the evil contained within escaped and spread over all the earth. She tried to close the lid but all the evil had escaped. Pandora was worried that she was going to get in big trouble over this, but Zeus did not punish Pandora because he knew in advance this would happen. Hopefully you can see the parallel between this tale and the story of the Garden of Eden. The mythologies literally run concurrent with the Biblical story, and the proponents of the Great Plan just keep telling them over and over and over, with all the same characters but new names and geographic locations.

Pan is also the mold from which the lesser 'satyrs' sprung out of, which are basically much less powerful forms of Pan, but with the same ½ man, ½ goat appearance. Satyrs in particular were the consorts of the Greek god Dionysus, known to the Romans as Bacchus, who is another version of King Nimrod along with Apollo. Bacchus is often depicted as having horns in ancient Roman art.

Something to remember when viewing all these ancient mythologies is that Satan and Nimrod are particularly self-important and take the form of many different gods in the ancient mythologies to span all the characteristics of their personalities. In the Greek mythology, Satan is Cronus/Pan/Hermes and more, and Nimrod is Zeus/Apollo/Dionysus and maybe more.

In fact, '**satyr**iasis' is uncontrollable or excessive sexual desire in a man, with its counterpart term '**nymph**omania' for a woman.

These terms are used today and are testament to the importance of sex in relation to the occult/supernatural.

The term 'satyr' is used in the Bible in place of the Hebrew 'se'irim' which means 'hairy ones', from the word 'sair' or 'goat'. The term 'satyr', which predates the term 'Saturn' that came into existence during the Roman Empire, is the origination of the term 'Saturn' to represent both the god and the planet.

Satyrs are acknowledged by name in the Book of Isaiah, who lived during the time of the peak of the Greek mythology that had been spread around the area:

> *"But wild beasts of the desert shall lie there; and their houses shall be full of doleful creatures; and owls shall dwell there, and satyrs shall dance there."*
> *-Isaiah 13:21 KJV*

> *"The wild beasts of the desert shall also meet with the wild beasts of the island, and the satyr shall cry to his fellow; the screech owl also shall rest there, and find for herself a place of rest."*
> *-Isaiah 34:14 KJV*

So. The image of Satan as we know him today is largely based upon the image of Baphomet by Satanist Eliphas Levi. Baphomet, the god of the Knights Templar, was based on 'Pan' the nature god of nearly two millennia earlier in ancient Greece, circa 800-700 BC. Pan was in turn based on an even more ancient depiction of Satan 1,400 years prior to the Greek empire in ancient Sumer/ Babylon called Capricorn. Capricorn was the image associated with the Sumerian god Enki, the first post-Flood representation of Satan.

Let's go all the way to ancient Sumer now and see how this got off the ground right after the Flood, and the Great Plan made its way down the line from Sumer to where we are today.

Chapter 5

TRUTH IN MYTH

"The devil, whose business is to pervert the truth, mimics the exact circumstances of the Divine Sacraments. He baptizes his believers and promises forgiveness of sins from the Sacred Fount, and thereby initiates them into the religion of Mithras. Thus he celebrates the oblation of bread, and brings in the symbol of the resurrection. Let us therefore acknowledge the craftiness of the devil, who copies certain things of those that be Divine."

-Tertullian

What is easier to put over on humanity? For Satan to try and flat out hide the truth, or to let it out but spin it as an exoteric myth, hiding the real truth behind it esoterically. The religion is exoteric, but the true meaning behind the religious/mythological system is exactly the **esoteric truth** contained in the occult secret societies, and it's exactly Satan worship.

It's quite ingenious actually. This same truth gets passed from empire to empire to empire, and this truth is if you want to rule the world, you have to worship Satan. **It's his world and he won't let you rule it unless it's through him**, and I honestly believe that to be a **fact.** This is how God set it up through His Divine Plan to test our eternal souls.

This is exactly why the Illuminati who run the world today are Satanists. They are receiving Satan's direct guidance to represent his interests on Earth in the divine game we are all a part of.

The ancient mythologies were the religious-political systems of their day, and their beliefs would encompass exactly the area of the empire it was heading, be it Sumer, Babylon, Greece, Rome or wherever. The common citizens were taught to worship those gods with all their heart and soul, their adoration, towards those pagan gods and it paid off for the elites who caused them to do that because the people were really worshipping Satan. This is exactly how it is today as you're going to see in chapter 6 concerning the modern day monotheistic faiths.

Many if not all ancient mythologies pay homage to exactly Satan, but we're just going to touch upon a few of the ones most significantly and glaringly proving that Satan's followers have set up all of the great mythologies and the empires that went with them of ancient history……. all the way to today. In the past they didn't hide worship of Satan, it was right out in the open, but after 2,000 years of suppression it seems it's coming back out into the open today if you're truly paying attention and 'awake'.

They used to do their ceremonies dedicated to Satan and Nimrod out in the open also. All those human sacrifices back in those days were done as public ceremonies, where today they are done behind closed doors and out of sight as a 'civilized' society as ours would not tolerate our leaders being involved with this. It used to be fine though, and even considered a great honor to be chosen to be a sacrifice to Satan, disguised as whatever the most powerful local deity was. In the case of the first recorded mythology in Sumer, that deity was called 'Enki'.

How in the world could a civilization literally come out of nowhere in ancient Sumer, and I'm quoting the archaeologists here, and ***immediately*** not only have the knowledge to build a civilization complete with language, government, religion, etc., but to start into the occult-Satanic practice of human sacrifice immediately???

Satan was surely responsible for the creation and introduction of the Sumerian mythology. He even has the starring role as Enki, and you're going to find this to be very interesting as we talk about how Satan tagged along with every major ancient mythology going forward. When Nimrod took it over from the Sumerian mythology, he reworked it and inserted himself.

This is the formula for nearly all ancient mythologies beginning with Nimrod: Azazel/Satan and King Nimrod/the Antichrist are the dominant members of all the pantheon of gods, typically occupying the personalities of multiple-gods, representing multiple characteristics of Satan and Nimrod. For instance, in this chapter, section C, we're going to see how Satan all by himself in the ancient Greek pantheon is represented chiefly as Cronus, but secondarily as Hephaestus, Prometheus, Hermes, Pan, Hades, Poseidon, and probably even more. In the Greek pantheon of gods, Nimrod is Zeus, Apollo, Dionysus and probably more. The female deities are based on the female deity of the Babylonian Mystery Religion, be it Semiramis, Ishtar, Eastre, Isis, Astarte, or whoever.

At this point in my research I believe Nimrod was what is called a 'Rephaim', which is the post-Flood equivalent of a Nephilim, and he would have been the first one. Partly divine, partly man, super-intelligent, larger than a typical man and very powerful physically.

This makes the most sense to me. The Rephaim existed in the ancient times according to the Bible, and by Satan procreating, fathering Nimrod, and then assigning divine-occult knowledge to Nimrod, he was able to organize and execute with precision the Great Plan in his day, setting the standard for Great Plan torch-bearers to come. Also, with Nimrod having divine-Satanic blood he would be eligible for worship as a ***demi-god***. As the hero depicted in the Epic of Gilgamesh from ancient Babylon, Nimrod is represented as part god and part man, **the exact definition of a Rephaim.** Gilgamesh is also often portrayed as being giant in size in ancient artwork, in one work holding a full-grown male lion in one arm as if it were a cat.

At this point in my research I also believe Nimrod is literally the son of Satan and that Satan/Azazel had once again transgressed into our dimension and mated with a woman, creating King Nimrod and his subsequent royal-bloodline-of-Satan Rephaim descendants, the venerable kings of the Earth.

It is also a theory of mine that Satan/Azazel was allowed back into our dimension physically as a ***woman***, the original female deity of the BMR to be exact. This would have made Satan King Nimrod's ***mother***, which might explain why it is said that he married his mother, and why all the reverence from the occultists for the female deity that has been recycled for millennia as the same being.

Now, the exact purpose of creating the mythologies is to put up a smoke screen to hide Satan and Nimrod as the true subjects of worship, but they are still able to receive adoration indirectly through their 'stand-ins'.

As a Rephaim, Nimrod would have had supernatural capabilities and after his death he would have been granted demon-status. He is currently in the Abyss with the 10% of the original pre-Flood Nephilim spirits Satan was granted as operatives according to the Book of Jubilees, another great extra-Biblical read. Nimrod is there now, the 'angel of the Abyss', where he is their king, inflicting their collective revenge on the human race for the fact that God wiped them all out in favor of the humans.

I'm going to show you how by reviewing the attributes and symbols of each individual god or even goddess, as they are recycled over and over and over down the line, it is not hard to figure out who is who in the ancient mythologies, or at least who they are intending to be paying homage to.

Chapter 5/A

ENKI/EA

It is my understanding that the very first image of Capricorn was actually of an antelope-fish, but that soon evolved into a goat-fish and has stayed the same ever since. This is the true origination of the goat symbology as representative for the one we call Satan today.

The time period that Capricorn represents in astrology is December 23 to January 20. Whose birthday falls in this time period again? King Nimrod. And of course also his 'savior son' Tammuz, both with birthdays on December 25, which, in astrological terms, is in the house of Capricorn (Enki/Satan), ruled over by the planet Saturn (Satan).

During the course of researching ancient Sumer and its associated mythology I found out even more stuff about the Great Plan for global enslavement that ultimately only buttressed my faith.

In my mind, all of the evidence about everything in general to do with religion, politics and the New World Order in general points **consistently** to the words of the Bible as truthful and having been inspired by God. If I felt otherwise I would certainly speak up about it.

I stated in my first book that virtually every major mythology and false religion has been spawned out of Nimrod's Babylonian Mystery Religion. I have since discovered that it appears that the basis of the BMR started ***before*** Nimrod in ancient Sumer and was subsequently taken over and revamped by Nimrod into a streamlined tyrannical enslavement machine to keep the Satanists perpetually in power.

Satan was in the Sumerian mythology pre-Nimrod by a few hundred years. Satan's character was kept (obviously) when Nimrod took over the area (Sumer) and its local religion, the Sumerian mythology. It was then incorporated into the Akkadian/ Babylonian mythology. Nimrod became known widely as Marduk and got Jupiter, Mars and the Sun as astrological representations. Satan/Enki became known as 'Ea' and took Saturn and Mercury as astrological representations. The female deities of Sumer were split between Venus and the Moon. Those were all the planets they knew about back then because that's all they could see as they hadn't invented telescopes just yet. There would have been no point incorporating planets they couldn't see into their astrological religious system, so they were left out back then. Azazel and the Watchers of course would have fully known about the other planets, but it would have been a moot point to early man to have 'invisible' planets/deities.

Aside from the multiple-deities, the stories surrounding the Sumerian mythology are very similar to the Bible and I have even found some things said in the Sumerian 'myth' that make sense when compared to what is in the Bible.

The reason the Bible and the Sumerian/Babylonian mythologies have story lines in common is because they are talking about the exact same stuff but with different authors and intentions.

The ancient myths and the Bible are relating many of the same things. The Establishment historians would have you believe that the Bible is merely a counterfeit of the Sumerian myths. I wholeheartedly disagree.

The mythologies conveniently don't tell us what ultimately happened to all these 'gods' and why they aren't around today if they were really all-powerful like they are made out to be. It seems the Bible and the extra-Biblical works like 1 Enoch ***do*** tell us what exactly happened to them: They are locked up in interdimensional prison, in the Abyss.

Before we even get into this section, I need to address discrepancies in the historical records concerning early mankind's history, and especially Mesopotamian (Sumer/Akkad/Babylon/etc.) history, as this is not only where mankind is alleged to have begun his time on Earth, but this is where the earliest known mythology comes from that ***all others are based on***, which is exactly the Sumerian mythology. There is much here that the proponents of the Great Plan would seek to muddy the waters over, as this particular mythology gives us big pieces of the whole New World Order-puzzle.

Again, I am quite sure that Mesopotamia rose ***after*** the Flood event and is not as old as the Establishment history books say it is, as the tumultuous actions of the Flood and the associated damage would have scrubbed clean virtually all traces of humanity except for something as massive and durable as the Great Pyramids.

There is something not quite lining up in my mind between the timeline of the Flood, of the establishment of Sumer according to popular history, and of the time Nimrod supposedly conquered all of Mesopotamia. I believe that Sumer is not as old of a settlement as we are told. In my mind, the Sumerian mythology had to have come right after the Flood, again because the Flood event is contained in the mythology. They can't have it both ways.

The ancient Sumerian mythology talks of a 'Golden Age' that preceded them, the exact same one the Greeks and Romans talked about in their mythologies that Cronus/Saturn ruled over, so we're all on the same page for sure when referring to the antediluvian times as the Golden Age when Azazel/Satan (who is the Sumerian god 'Enki' and Greek/Roman god Cronus/Saturn) and the Watchers (the Sumerian Annunaki) ruled over the land.

So it seems that immediately after the Flood event, this preassembled religious system based on astrology came out of nowhere and was set up with a starring role for Satan as 'Lord of the Earth', the Sumerian god Enki.

If Satan was not going to control the world himself in person, he would control it with a stand-in. What appears to have happened is that people immediately started worshipping the most important pagan god from before the Flood, namely Satan, who was characterized by 'them' as Enki. A bunch of other characters were added to muddy up the water, including what looks to be our Heavenly Father as the chief god over Enki, named **Anu**. This is why the Annunaki are called what they are in the Sumerian mythology. The 'sons of God' from Genesis are the 'sons of Anu' in the Sumerian myth, the Annunaki.

So. Capricorn was a representation of Enki, and this is the origination of the horned-god symbology related to Azazel/Satan and also even Nimrod. 'Capri' means goat. The 'corn' part of the word Capricorn means 'horn'. This is where the ***Unicorn*** (one horn) gets its name, the one-horned magical horse. The term 'cornucopia' translates to 'horn of plenty'. Again, this is why the devil has horns. Horns are also meant to be representative of divinity in ancient mythology and artwork.

Enki was also the first 'serpent god', with one of his symbols being the caduceus, which is two intertwined snakes. The caduceus arguably looks like it was meant to resemble a strand of DNA---about 4,500 years ago no less. This goes hand-in-hand with Enki's apparent role as a DNA engineer---the reason he got in so much trouble with God and caused the Flood. The only ones who could know what a DNA strand looked like back then would have been exactly God or His agents/employees/angels.... including Enki/Azazel/Satan.

It is the mastery of DNA technology which will bring the Great Plan to a climax, with the resurrection of King Nimrod, remember? That is what the serpent represents, knowledge, and ultimately the knowledge to gain mastery of using advanced DNA technology to not only bring back Nimrod but to activate the supernatural aspects contained in all humans. Ever heard of 'transhumanism'? There's something for you to look into.

The Sumerian religion was probably 'given' to the Sumerians not long after mankind began to repopulate after the Flood. Ancient Sumer is the origin of all snake worship throughout global history. This is why Satan is referred to as a serpent in the Garden of Eden in the Bible, which was written over a thousand years after the Sumerian mythology was created.

Enki's dedicated city in ancient Sumer was called Eridu, and it was the most important and largest city in the entire Sumerian empire. According to archaeologists, the largest and oldest ziggurat they have ever found was constructed in Eridu.

It is possible that the Tower of Babel was in Eridu, and others more knowledgeable than I on this topic have hypothesized this also. This would make sense for sure, as Satan would have wanted the ultimate dedication to be to him, the 'Lord of the Earth'. By having the tallest and largest religious structure around at the time as a dedication to him in his dedicated town, Eridu

One last bullet point here about Enki, and that is the ancient Sumerian work called ***'Enki and the World Order'.*** It is what is called a narrative poem, and basically heaps the praises of mankind and the other gods upon Enki in very generous servings, and what a great god he is, etc. etc. ad nauseum.

This is probably where the term '***New*** World Order' originated. The **New World Order** is the attempt at reviving the **Golden Age** when Satan/Enki/Cronus/Saturn/Azazel and his minions ruled the land **exoterically**, not **esoterically** like they do today. As you can see globally now, all this stuff is starting to come out into the open, Satan is not hiding anymore.

It seems we are not far away at all from the Satanists ruling **exoterically** once again.......

Chapter 5/B

SATURN WORSHIP

As history ticked away from Sumer onward, it ultimately came about that Saturn worship, which is Satan worship, and the Babylonian Mystery Religion, which is Antichrist worship, were to be the veiled control structures of the empires the Satanists ran.

Satan became associated with the planet Saturn, but not until he had fine-tuned how he wanted the mythologies to be set up. Beginning in the ancient Sumerian mythology as the god Enki, Satan was then adapted into the Babylonian mythology, the one Nimrod had control of, as the god 'Ea'. Ninurta was the Saturn-designated god in Sumer, but Enki was also associated with Saturn through Capricorn.

Shamash in the Sumerian mythology is also associated with Saturn. Satan wasn't considered to be fully represented by the planet Saturn until after the Babylonian Mystery Religion had migrated to ancient Egypt and Canaan, with Canaan specifically being the land of the post-Flood giants, the Rephaim from the Old Testament. The angel-human hybrids from before the Flood were called the Nephilim, in the days after the Flood when they came back into existence were now referred to as the Rephaim.

The Rephaim in Canaan and elsewhere were the offspring of Rephan. Rephan is another name for Saturn in the ancient world. The Rephaim were literally the descendants of Satan...or children, grandchildren, etc. most likely via Nimrod/the Antichrist. Once again they were on the Earth like before the Flood, causing mankind all kinds of trouble. All those times the ancient Israelis had to fight the giants, it was exactly God's people vs. exactly Satan's people in hand to hand combat!

The existence of these aptly-named Rephaim giants seems to suggest that Azazel/Satan was let out, or **busted out,** of jail via an occult/supernatural ceremony to procreate once again on Earth.

In ancient Canaan, Assyria, and surrounding areas, Enki/Ea became known as the god 'El' and was represented by the planet Saturn. El's son, 'Baal', was another representation of Nimrod and was the Sun god, with his wife the Moon god Asherah/Astarte/Ashtoreth/Ishtar/Semiramis.

> *"Saturn is the opposite to Jupiter; his symbol is the cross above the sign of Luna. He is the Satan, the Tempter, or rather the Tester. His function is to chastise and tame the unruly passions in the primitive man."*
>
> *- J.S. Ward, 'Freemasonry and the Ancient Gods*

We're going to fast forward now to much closer to our times, the universally well-known pantheon of gods represented in ancient Greece.

Chapter 5/C

CRONUS IN GREECE

As you know it would take voluminous amounts of space to cover every single ancient mythology and break them down. I've given you the beginning and told you about the middle, so we're going to wrap it up with the end of the mythological line, which is Greece and Rome.

The Greek mythology changed up the story of Azazel as revealed in 1 Enoch, but we are still talking the exact same scenario: gods, giants, gods having sex with humans and creating demigod offspring, and crazy, mixed-DNA/DNA corrupted species of animals and animal/human hybrids. Ever heard of a centaur? How about a minotaur? These hybrids may well have existed at one point for real. They are doing experiments today using human-animal mixtures in high-tech labs. We are re-living the 'days of Noah' right now it seems.

Now, it is interesting but not surprising to note that the Greek mythology mirrors the Sumerian mythology and others in that there is a Creator God or gods over the head of Cronus/Saturn/Azazel/Satan/whoever, which is just the mythologies mirroring the truth that Satan certainly is not the most powerful being in existence but a subordinate.

The Greek legend goes that Cronus overthrew ***his*** father, arguably a representation of the Most High, and ruled over what is called the Golden Age of mankind, the same antediluvian Golden

Age in the Sumerian mythology referring to the pre-Flood world, and the same described in detail in 1 Enoch.

Again, what we call the antediluvian world the occultists call Atlantis. Cronus was the designated ruler of the mythological Atlantis, or one of his stand-ins as we will go over, depending on what researcher says what. Poseidon was also said to rule over Atlantis, but Poseidon is just another representation of Satan in my opinion. There are many gods within each mythology that represent Satan and Nimrod.

The Greek story progresses that Cronus' son Zeus overthrows ***him***, imprisons him in Tartarus (the Abyss) and takes over the Earth. This represents the transition between the pre-Flood and post-Flood worlds, with Zeus representing Nimrod taking up the reigns in the physical world for the now Abyss-imprisoned Cronus/ Azazel. Zeus is represented as the planet Jupiter in the Greek and other mythologies, including all the way back to the Akkadian Empire/Babylon when Nimrod first appeared in the mythologies as Marduk.

Cronus is nearly always depicted in ancient Greek art as holding a scythe, which is a large sickle used for harvesting grain. This original image of Cronus holding the scythe was then mutated into another character who was to be specifically associated with Cronus, and that is **'Father Time'**.

Yes, Father Time is really a variation of Satan. The god 'Cronus', also spelled 'Chronus', is where we get the term 'chronology' today, which means 'time'. Cronus is regarded as the 'god of time' in the Greek mythology, and this is why Father Time holds a scythe.

The image of **Death**, the skeleton-looking, black-cloaked figure carrying the ***scythe*** who comes around when it's time to die **is also factually based on Cronus.**

Since the Book of Revelation was written during the time that everybody knew about these characters, including the character of Death and that his alias was Cronus (Saturn when the Book of Revelation was given by Jesus to His servant John of Patmos) and who he really was, **Satan,** this sheds new light on this verse from Revelation:

> *"And I looked, and behold a pale horse: and his ***name *** that sat on him was ***Death***, and Hell followed with him. And power was given unto them over the fourth part of the earth, to kill with sword, and with hunger, and with death, and with the beasts of the earth."*
>
> *-Book of Revelation, 6:8 (KJV)*

Now, there are other gods in the Greek pantheon who I believe are meant to be representations of different characteristics of Satan, and we'll briefly go over these now along with their characteristics/symbology that is attached to them.

It is my opinion that Satan is not only Cronus, but his unique characteristics are also spread out among Atlas, Hyperion, Oceanus, Prometheus, Pan, Hades, Poseidon and Hermes.....and possibly more but this is enough to make my case.

To start with, Atlas, who is Cronus' nephew, is one of the 'lesser' Titans compared to Cronus. He is depicted as the 'strong god' who holds up the heavens. Azazel translated to English equals roughly 'strong one of God' or 'God strengthens'. Atlas is also where the terms 'Atlantis' and 'Atlantic Ocean' are said to have come from.

Next we have Hyperion, who was a brother of Cronus, and the **father** of the Greek 'trinity' of Helios (Sun), Selene (Moon) and Eos (Dawn). This equates to Nimrod (Sun), Semiramis (Moon) and Tammuz (the Sun reborn as the dawn). Apollo is also a Sun god in the Greek mythology, and along with both Helios and Eos are representations of King Nimrod just to keep things straight here.

Oceanus is another brother of Cronus and a spinoff of the old Capricorn symbology, being half-man with horns and either half-serpent or half-fish. Just as Enki/Ea of the old Sumerian/Babylonian mythology, he is associated with water.

Prometheus, a lesser Titan and another of Cronus' nephews, was credited with creating mankind out of clay. Then he got in trouble for stealing fire (occult knowledge) from the Olympus gods and giving it to mankind. Sound familiar? Fire in this case signifies knowledge, occult knowledge. Prometheus was punished for this by Zeus for giving mankind what was reserved for the gods, and was chained to the side of a mountain, having his liver ripped out every day from a marauding giant eagle.

The eagle that attacks Prometheus daily is later slain by Hercules, yet another representation of Nimrod, and his chains are released. There are layers of stories upon stories in the ancient mythologies, but the original two characters remain the same even if they are at odds or competing against each other in the story line.

We already went over the Greek god **Pan** so we'll move on to Hades, who is the son of Cronus and brother of Zeus and Poseidon. Hades is king of the underworld (under the Earth where Azazel's physical body was contained per 1 Enoch) that is named after him, and the 'god of the dead', mirroring Cronus alter-ego 'Death'. His **3-headed** (unholy trinity) dog Cerberus is in his constant service.

Poseidon is just another spin off of Enki/Ea. Poseidon is nearly always pictured wielding the trident, which is a **3-pronged** spear, which in turn of course again probably represents the unholy trinity as a weapon of Satan against us. This is why in today's images of Satan he wields the trident from the 'fires of Hell', even though the trident is a ***maritime*** weapon. Why would Satan wield what is basically a glorified fish spear? You already know the answer.

Hermes immediately grabbed my attention in my studies because his symbol is the caduceus. Hermes name is also incorporated in many occult themes, including **Herme**tic alchemy.

Now it was ***Apollo*** who is said to have given ***Hermes*** the caduceus as a gesture of friendship no less, explaining how Hermes came to have the caduceus symbolically represent him in the Greek mythology, but we know this symbol all the way back from Sumer now. The names change but the symbols stay the same for Satan, just as he has been dragging around the hexagram for thousands of years to this day.

Apollo went on to have a son named Asclepius, whose symbol was known as the single staff with a snake. It is my understanding that the Staff of Asclepius was used as the modern-day symbol for medicine, but people are always getting it confused with the caduceus, so now they are both equated to being about the same these days by society, and unknowingly they're not far from the truth.

The Greeks were a very interesting people, with a highly advanced society for the time, highly sophisticated and intelligent.... and completely morally corrupt. Human sacrifice was written about in the mythology but due to the advancement of their society was largely taken underground by the elites running the show. It is said, however, that babies were indeed sacrificed to Cronus in Greece as they had been previously in ancient Canaan/Assyria/Carthage. Babies in particular were sacrificed to Cronus because according to the mythology he ate his own children as they were born so they wouldn't overthrow him like he did his father, Uranus.

When those ancient times (pre-Greece) got tough and the people were starving, they felt they needed to appease Cronus in particular, the god of agriculture, and the children were sacrificed. This was most evident in ancient Carthage, where again a bronze statue was used as the sacrificial murder device. This time instead of Moloch it was Cronus, and again the metal statue was heated and the children were placed in the red-hot hands of the idol to suffer a torturous death. Often hundreds of children would be killed in a single ceremony in ancient Carthage.

Public human sacrifice might have been largely taken off the table beginning in ancient Greece, but sexual perversion and pedophilia were normalized and were the order of the day in the ancient Greek society.

Back in ancient Greece, chiefly during the Archaic and Classical periods stemming from around 800 B.C. to 280 B.C., ***it was con-***

sidered societally-acceptable for men to take young, pre-pubescent or adolescent males under their wing and show them everything about homosexual relations.

This was called 'pederasty'......

The two Greek gods who are most representative of Nimrod, **Zeus and Apollo,** are cited as having engaged in sodomizing young boys (in the mythology of course). Google 'Apollo Hyacinth', 'Apollo Cyparissus', and 'Zeus Ganymede' for the Greek mythological stories about this.

The Bible tells us this about Nimrod/the Antichrist in particular:

> *"He will show no regard for the gods of his fathers or for the desire of women, nor will he show regard for any other god; for he will magnify himself above them all."*
> *-Book of Daniel, 11:37*

The reason the Antichrist won't desire the company of women is because he is a sexual deviant to the extreme, you won't find any worse. All he desires sexually is male-on-male-child sodomy. I know that sounds disgusting and reprehensible, but I believe it to be the truth. These sex rituals will help the Antichrist harness the power of Satan himself just like Satan's followers do today.

Chapter 5/D

SATURN IN ROME

Now we come to the Roman Empire, which was the next empire in line for the Great Plan right after the fall of Greece. Since everyone was worshipping the Greek gods anyways, the Romans just took over the Greek pantheon, kept all the same gods but renamed them, and called them theirs.

If the Greek Empire had continued, we would be calling what we know as the planet Saturn, 'Cronus', the planet Jupiter would be 'Zeus' and so on and so forth, and it would seem completely normal to us.

Ancient Rome was nicknamed the 'City of Saturn', and this was because the city of Rome was located right where the even older city of Saturnia existed. Saturnia dates from the 4th century BC and prior.

In the Book of Revelation, the seven heads/mountains are typically identified with Rome, which was the nickname of Rome back when the NT was written and known as the 'city of seven hills'.

The smallest of these hills in Rome was called **'Capitoline Hill'**, which is where the Roman seat of government was located, and this is where the term **'Capitol Hill'** comes from in Washington DC. Capitoline Hill in Rome was exactly Satan's installed government and Capitol Hill here in Washington D.C. that rules over the New Babylon, the USA, is also Satan's installed government.

Their biggest festival of the year in Rome during Jesus' day was called Saturnalia, and it was held during our 'Christmas season'.

There is a bunch of information about this Roman holiday that you can look up for yourself to save page space here, but it was quite a raucous party to be sure.

Since ancient Rome was completely under the evil ones' control, evil reigned. The ancient blood sports held in the Roman Coliseum when Jesus was here in the flesh were absolutely unbelievable. They had all manners of exotic animals at their disposal. Elephants. Lions. Tigers. You name it. In one documented day of bloodletting, over 9,000 of these magnificent animals were brutally slaughtered in the Coliseum to the delight of the crowd. Look up 'bestiari' and 'venatores', who were respectively prisoners and volunteers who would fight against animals in the Coliseum to the death. The Coliseum games were the ancient form of our more-civilized-society's football, baseball and other assorted games that took the place of the ancient blood sports per the 'Report from Iron Mountain'.

These were the times that upstanding characters like Julius Caesar, Caligula and the like ruled Rome. Sadistic. Bloodthirsty. Sexually perverted to the worst possible degree. Bloodthirsty. They were the stand-ins for Nimrod of their day and their evil knew no bounds.

Satanists ruled Rome before Jesus came and after He was gone and it was exactly their kind that took over Christianity nearly right out of the gate. The Roman Empire kept the Great Plan going and morphed the blossoming worship of Jesus with Mithraism and the Roman mythology, creating Roman Catholicism. Many books besides mine have been written about this exact scenario that is the truth.

This is why there are massive problems with the Catholic Church via homosexual abuse of young Catholic boys by their elders since its inception all the way to today. It has always been like this since the days of Nimrod. These same types of people were now at the helm of the new 'Christian' religion.

It was all downhill from there as they have trashed God's and Jesus' reputation all the way down the line. Do you really think Jesus would have approved of the Inquisition? Sexual torture of innocent people??? Rampant pedophilia???

The god Saturn is exactly where we get the name of the seventh day of the week of the Gregorian calendar we use today: ***Saturday.*** This is also the day of worship for Judaism and you will soon see why. Sunday is the designated day to worship the Sun/Nimrod/ Antichrist. Saturday is to worship Saturn/Azazel/Satan. The real Sabbath was originally a constantly-changing day based on lunar cycles.

The real Sabbath has then, in effect, been lost to the true faith. I define 'true faith' as that which existed during and right after Jesus' time here in person, that which was corrupted by the ancient Romans with symbols, imagery, holidays, etc. I'm currently looking into this very important matter and will get back to you in my next book, the third of this series I'm creating to help people better understand all aspects of the New World Order, especially the spiritual-supernatural end of it.

Chapter 6

OCCULT SYMBOLISM

*"Symbolism is the language of the Mysteries (***Great Plan***) ... By symbols men have ever sought to communicate to each other those thoughts which transcend the limitations of language. Rejecting man-conceived dialects as inadequate and unworthy to perpetuate divine ideas, the Mysteries (***Great Plan***) thus chose symbolism as a far more ingenious and ideal method of preserving their transcendental knowledge. In a single figure a symbol may both reveal and conceal, for to the wise the subject of the symbol is obvious, while to the ignorant the figure remains inscrutable. Hence, he who seeks to unveil the secret doctrine of antiquity must search for that doctrine not upon the open pages of books which might fall into the hands of the unworthy but in the place where it was originally concealed."*

-33rd Degree Freemason Manly P. Hall, from his book 'The Secret Teachings of All Ages'

I've got a question for you:

"What are the odds that the company with the symbol for the *exact representation* of the 'Fall of Man' as their official logo since their inception would go on to be the most valuable company in the world?"

That company was Apple Computer. Their logo, the apple with a bite taken out of it, certainly could be interpreted as representing man eating the fruit of the Tree of Knowledge and advancing towards godhood on Earth.

In late 2014, Apple, Inc. became the first company to be valued at over **$700 billion**, making it the most valuable company in the history of mankind. And their logo just happens to be a single image that corrals and encompasses exactly the Great Plan? Of mankind seeking knowledge (technology) along the path to becoming an immortal?

Pardon the pun, but was Apple ***picked*** to be one of the torchbearers for the Great Plan of advancing man's technological capabilities? Or were they marked for success because they were inviting in otherworldly help with their occult **symbol?**

Whether the founders of Apple intended it or not, Satan and his demonic host are attracted to symbols that can call upon and welcome their interference in our world. This is exactly why symbols are used in Satanic ceremonies, such as the pentagram and hexagram. They are virtually a 'seal of approval' from the humans that the evil ones have our permission to come and interact with whoever is presenting those symbols.

By Apple, Inc. using the particular symbol they did, they arguably attracted the attention of Satan himself to take that company with that exact logo for the Great Plan and advance them to the top, which is exactly what happened.

How about the **#2** most valuable company in the history of mankind, **Exxon.**

'Exxon' the name contains the symbol of Satan himself in it as you will soon see here. Another coincidence? How about Microsoft? Do you see that Internet Explorer logo on your screen? The one that is a representation of **Saturn** once you fill in all the blue on the 'e'? Occult symbology is all over the biggest corporations in the world and it's exactly because they are trying to enlist the help of the supernatural.

Symbols are all around us all the time no matter where we are, and they certainly get our attention. Symbols give direction to those who know what they represent. The occult symbols we're going to go over are more than just shapes to be sure. They originated in mankind's ancient history and give directions to the operatives of the New World Order.

I had reservations about sharing with you what we're going to go over because you're never going to be able to look around you the same way ever again, especially the symbol of the Christian cross. The cross is the globally-accepted **symbol** for Christianity to those who don't know what it ***really*** represents.

Unfortunately, the symbol of the cross not only originated in the occult, but it originated as exactly a Satanic symbol. Just like the holidays are truly Satanic, paying homage to the Antichrist King Nimrod and by default Satan, the cross is originally a symbol for Nimrod and Nimrod-reborn on December 25 as Tammuz. The cross was originally called a Tau, named after Tammuz. In ancient Babylon. Just because people ***believe*** it represents Jesus does not make it so any more than believing that Christmas is really about Jesus and not the Antichrist. This all goes back to what Jesus told us about loving God with our ***minds, not our eyes.*** This is exactly why God forbids any images of anything Divine in the Ten Commandments.

We have been under a constant deception ever since we got here on Earth around 4000 BC, and very, very few have been able to see through this deception, understand it, and warn others exactly what is going on. This is precisely what the prophets did for God back in the day. That's what the Bible is: God's 'called' people telling His followers exactly what's going on, even if it's bad news they just don't want to hear or abide by, let alone accept as bare-bones truth.

How many times did God's prophets call out the ancient Israelis and Judahites for straying, calling them 'a rebellious people'? It seems, as a whole, they were on the naughty list more often than not in the Bible. They were only rebellious in God's eyes though, as all the societies around them had been mired in the Satanic Matrix forever, and they were just joining the crowd basically. When the ancient Israelis strayed it was just over to the side of 'general society' at the time.

It seems that most of our fellow brethren are in this exact spot today: Following the Satanic holidays, displaying the Satanic symbols, worshipping on Satanically-designated days, chasing money, fame, power. etc. Most of the brethren seem to only step out of the Satanic Matrix for one hour, one day a week.......and it's on the wrong day.

Now, the only way the Great Plan can work is if a small, secretive group of people are controlling it. Not everybody can be the boss on this planet; you need bosses who give direction and workers who execute it. In today's world, the Illuminati are happy to assume the boss role, but they have to prove they are worthy to Satan himself and that's where the occult symbols and ceremonies come in.

When the Great Plan got up and running again in ancient Sumer after the Flood, the proponents of the Great Plan needed occult symbols in order to network. These ancient symbols meant different things to different people. The meanings of the symbols were different to the occultists as opposed to the general population. Satan's people understood the exoteric meaning **and** the esoteric meaning, but the public-at-large were only meant to understand the exoteric meaning, which is whatever they were told it meant at the time. The exoteric meaning changes from empire to empire, **but the original esoteric meaning never changes.** This is why they recycle the same symbols over and over. The meaning only changes for the deceived, never for the deceivers.

This is why today people are calling the 'Star of Rephan/ Saturn' the 'Star of David'. Most people have no idea the hexagram is representative of Satan himself.

Symbols are hugely important to the people running the Great Plan. They didn't have smart phones back then, so they needed to be able to communicate with each other secretly but have their message out where other occultists could see it and know that whatever it was attached to was part of the plan, the Great Plan.

Well my friend, there's not really a 'correct' order to what we're going to go over, other than I tried to categorize the occult symbolism world the best I could. Truly the only way to be considered an 'expert' on the symbolism we're going to go over is to be an insider to the operations of the Illuminati, which I am obviously not.

I think I did a well enough job to get you at least pointed in the right direction. There is such a vast body of information about the New World Order it can be overwhelming and it ***was before*** I got saved and everything came into focus. We're just beginning to ramp up a supernatural battle of Biblical proportions and most people don't know the magnitude of what's happening and what's coming just yet, but you certainly do and will know even more as we go forward together in my works.

It is possible that there are even more meanings for the symbols we're going to review, or maybe a debate about my interpretation of one or more. My ears are open on anything in this section, this chapter, this book. All of it. Anything at all. I welcome open discussion about anything and everything I'm talking about. We're all adults here, this certainly isn't a kid's book. There is nothing in this book people should be afraid to talk about because it's all based on the truthful facts as always.

God wants the people who actively seek it to know the truth about the very things we're talking about, and that is why you are here with me right now, at this point, in this book:

You seek the truth.

Chapter 6/A

SACRED GEOMETRY

"The most incomprehensible thing about the universe is that it is comprehensible."
-Albert Einstein

Sacred geometry is all around us, all the time. These are the geometric shapes and patterns that our 3D world is constructed of. The very reason geometry is 'sacred' to the occultists is that these shapes and assemblies of shapes originated from the Divine blueprint of how our world operates.

Sacred geometry is found everywhere in our existence, from going from a thought to physical form as a bee makes a honeycomb from perfect hexagons, from a snowflake which always manifests as a hexagonal/6-sided shape, all the way to the very building blocks of life at the subatomic level, which again are typically 6-sided in shape. Our entire universe is made of these building blocks that the ancients immortalized as symbols for the Great Plan, specifically because they are symbols of the 3D world that Satan lords over. They are his symbols because this is his world.

The ancients have left us a plethora of evidence that those running the New World Order way back then knew of sacred geometry and put it in designs on everything, from symbols such as the Seed/Fruit/Tree of life to the symbols of the pentagram, hexagram, etc. that are used in black magic/occult rituals.

Not only did the ancient occultists know things that the general population is just now finding out through advancements in science, but by them being shown how to hack into God's natural system by Satan/Azazel and the Watchers way back in the pre-Flood days, they were and are able to obtain even more occult information, prognosis of the future even in my opinion. It's just like they're hacking into God's computer network, with the ways to do this having been passed down over the millennia by the ever-regenerating proponents of the Great Plan. Those ways are exactly the gruesome Satanic blood and sex rituals they perform in honor of ***their*** god, Satan.

Sacred geometry has been incorporated into the designs of religious structures of all walks of life, buildings, towns and even entire cities. One look at the street map of Washington D.C. and it's not hard to see that it's laid out according to the occult and many have already made the case showing that it is in fact laid out incorporating occult sacred geometry. Virtually every significant federal building in Washington DC has a Masonic plaque on it, from Washington Monument to the George Washington Memorial, so this should not be a surprise at all around ***Capitoline*** **Hill**.

Sacred geometry has been turned into religious symbols of all types, appearing on religious structures, art, stained glass, amulets, necklaces, bracelets, rings, clothes, and all the rest of it. In other words, it's everywhere you turn and always has been...... just like the followers of Satan.

Chapter 6/B

SATURN SYMBOLISM

It was exactly my finding out that the symbol of the 'Sigil of Saturn' is also the occult symbol of Azazel that sent me down the path to write a book about Satan. I had known a little about Saturn worship but hadn't yet really looked into it. I'd heard that Satan and the ancient pagan god Saturn were one and the same, but had no idea how it could be construed as that.

I found it intriguing that Azazel from 1 Enoch would share a symbol with the ancient occult 'god' Saturn. I had a hunch that Azazel was Satan after the first reading of 1 Enoch, so I started looking into exactly who 'Azazel' was.

Every time I would start looking into Azazel that same Sigil of Saturn would make an appearance, invariably leading me into looking into Saturn worship. The reason Azazel and Saturn kept popping up together is of course that it turns out that Azazel ***is*** the god Saturn, and the reason they shared the same symbol was that they were the same being but with different names from different groups of people. Once I came to that conclusion I re-read 1 Enoch and it made so much more sense knowing that Azazel ***was*** the missing 'Satan' I had wondered about when I had first read it.

Now you know the real story, that **Satan = Azazel = Saturn = Cronus = Enki**, and he has been here the whole time we have.

I'm going to go over something now, and this is a **truly** incredible 'coincidence': For the first time ever, NASA received images from the Voyager space mission in 1982 clear enough of Saturn to see something absolutely amazing......

There was a stationary, ever-perpetuating storm system at the north pole of Saturn, and it was shaped exactly like a **hexagon**. This is a huge storm, with each side of this hexagonal anomaly measuring approximately **7,500 miles long**.

This is an absolutely huge, perfect-shaped hexagon, and this is a seemingly odd situation until you figure in the hand of the god of this world, Satan.

The people running the ancient-end of the Great Plan had to have known about this natural or possibly supernaturally-based giant hexagon covering Saturn's North Pole.

The odds of a naturally occurring giant hexagonal-shape on Saturn and Saturn in particular, are incalculable.

Here is a direct quote from Madame Blavatsky's 'Isis Unveiled':

> *"It may be easily proved that from time immemorial Saturn or Kronos, whose ring, most positively was discovered by the Chaldean astrologers, and whose symbolism is no "coincidence,".....*

She is claiming here that the symbolism for Saturn (hexagram/all-seeing eye in particular) came from ancient Chaldean astrologers.

According to the accepted scientific-societal norm, the rings of Saturn were discovered in 1610 AD, not by ancient Chaldean astrologers in the BC era, with 'Chaldean' equating to Babylonian.

No one knows how this hexagonal-storm is possible. Not the national weather service. Not the Establishment-University astronomers/professors. Not even NASA can explain the existence of the rings around Saturn let alone a true hexagon on the surface of its North Pole. Do you know who does know for sure what is up with this storm, the rings, and everything else to do with their beloved Saturn, which is the esoteric representation of Satan?

The Illuminati.

This is the kind of occult information that gets passed down through the secret societies.

It is my opinion that two separate and ancient symbols for the god Saturn have come out of this hexagonal marking on Saturn. One is the infamous ***hexagram*** you are already familiar with, and another is the ***cube***, and in particular a **black cube**. A hexagon to the occultists is equated with a 3D-image of a cube. The cube in the occult world is representative of not only Saturn the god but our 3D world that he is the god of.

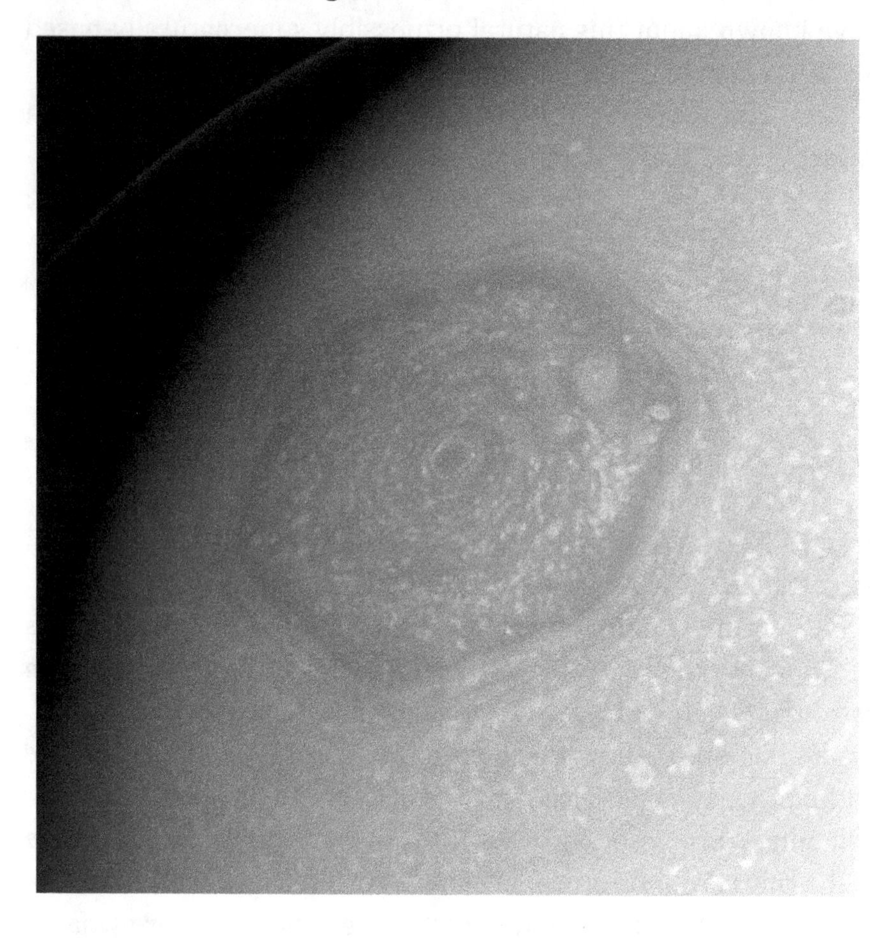

North Pole of Saturn as taken by space mission Cassini

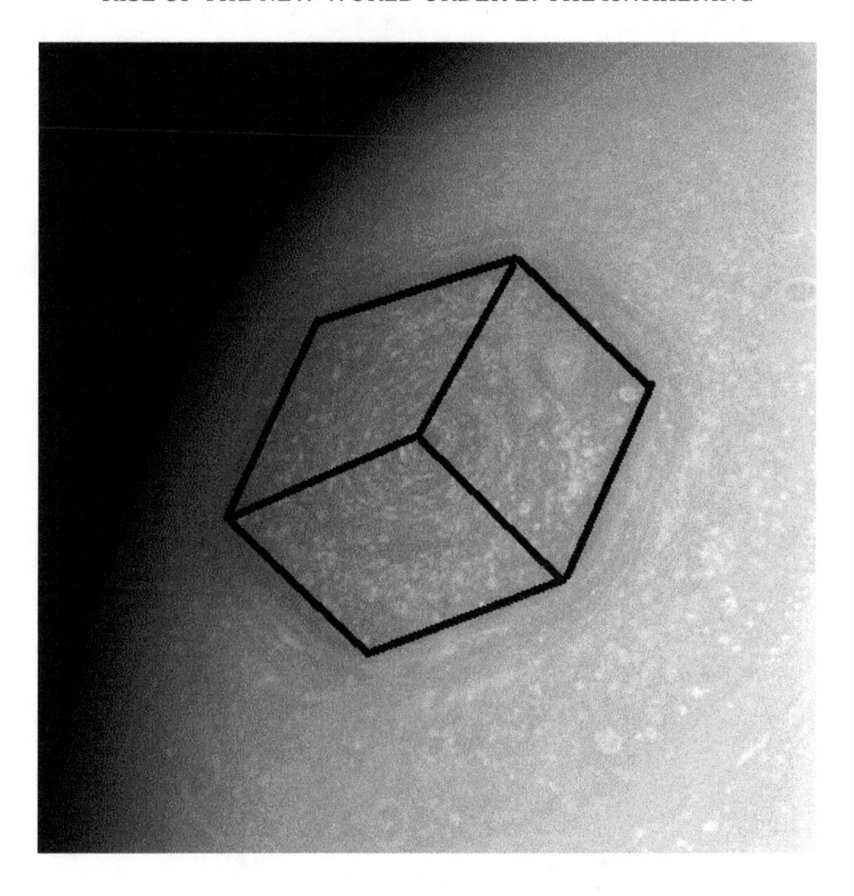

Diagram of a 3D cube that is derived from a hexagon

There is even a third occult symbol that I believe is due to a physical feature of Saturn, and it's not the hexagonal storm at Saturn's north pole. That feature is the ***OTHER*** storm on Saturn, the one at the ***SOUTH*** Pole, that looks like the infamous 'all- seeing eye'.

These physical anomalies on Saturn were here vastly longer than the human race and there are only seldom coincidences in this realm of research with regards to issues like this.

Here is arguably the real origination of the symbol of the all-seeing eye. Note in the image below, the **oblong, eye-like appearance** of literally the ***eye of the storm covering the South Pole of Saturn***:

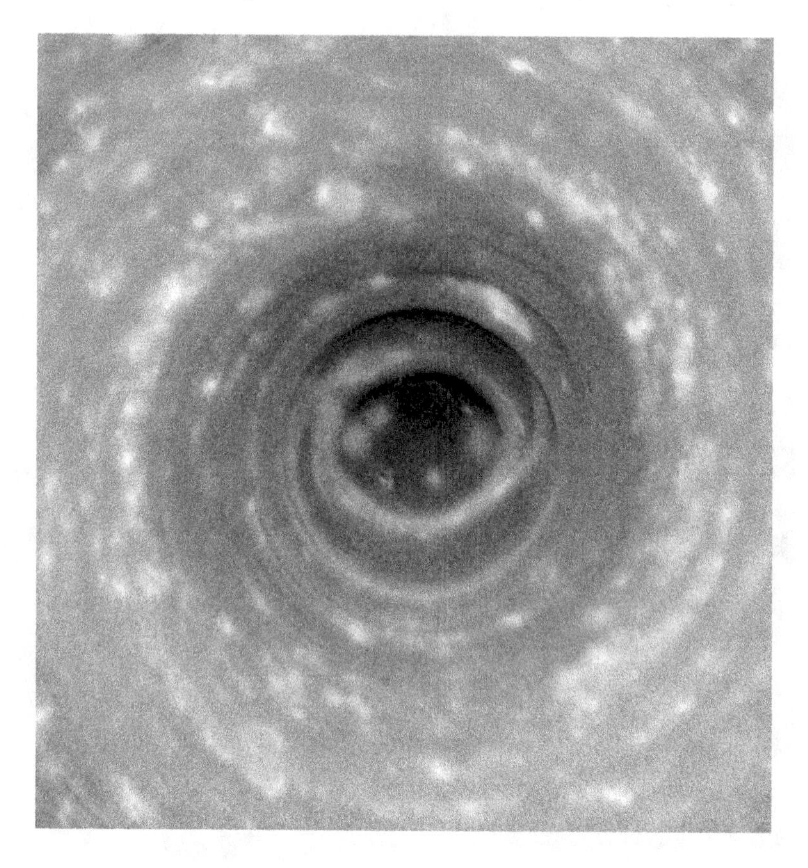

Image of the South Pole of Saturn as taken by space mission Cassini

Sometimes the all-seeing eye is depicted as radiating light out. This could be one of two things. One would be the light representing occult knowledge, radiating from Saturn/Azazel/Satan to his followers. **The other would be the fact that Saturn isn't a planet but is actually a small sun!** Saturn is factually a sun, classified as a 'brown dwarf star'. Jupiter is a sun also, and I never knew or understood that to be true in all my years in the public education system, only learning this through the research for this book. I'm sure Satan let his people know, however.

Either way, the all-seeing eye is certainly representative of Saturn/ Satan, the god of the occult and this world, and **not** representative of the Most High, who is our God. When the Freemasons say the all-seeing eye = the 'eye of providence/god', they mean ***their*** god, Saturn.

Now, like I said earlier, the Sigil of Saturn and the occult sign for Azazel are the same symbol, and the symbol originates from something called the ***Magic Square of Saturn***. This is exactly a tool used in black magic to create what are called 'sigils', which uses numerology to create symbols for interacting with the supernatural.

The Magic Square of Saturn is also the same occult system as the Chinese **Lo Shu Square**, and this magical numerical system is all over the ancient world. The Magic Square of Saturn is the first and smallest of what are called 'magic squares' and this has to do with the occult.

The Magic Square of Saturn is a 3x3 grid, with the numbers 1 through 9 inserted in a particular order so that any consecutive 3-digit line when added together equals 15. The number 15 is therefore representative of Saturn in the occult, and this is also why in a deck of Tarot cards the Devil is card #15.

Here is what the **'Freemasonic Magic Square of Saturn'** looks like:

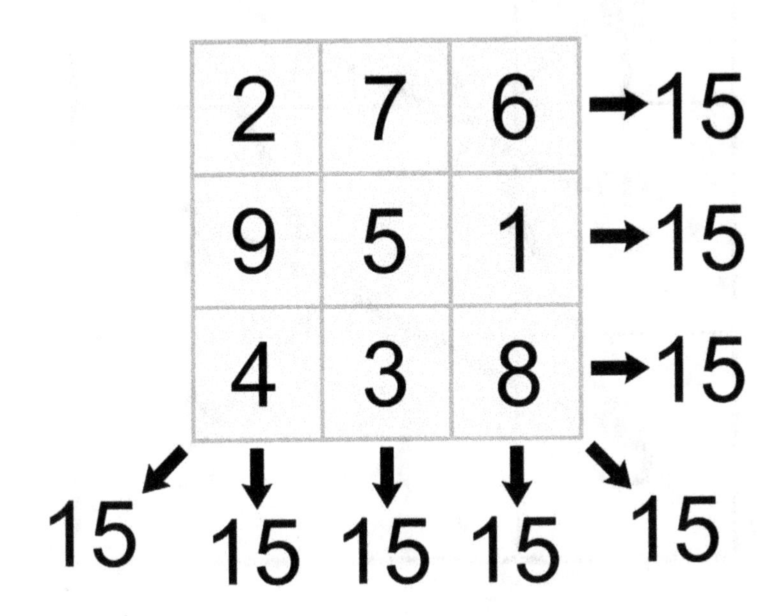

What we're going to go over now has to do with how to use the Magic Squares in black magic rituals and it is OK for you to hear this in the context of our studies. There are letter-to-number conversions I've seen that you would translate what you wanted to accomplish from the letters of the words of the wish into numbers, and then trace those numbers in order over the magic square, and that would be the symbol you would present to Satan or another demonic entity for them to help you fulfill your wish. This is literally inviting them into our reality to help you accomplish your goal. When you actively seek to enlist the power of the Devil and his associates they are attracted to this, a willing subject, and this is why this works to start with.

The occult symbols created in this way are called 'sigils' or 'seals'. The 'Sigil of Saturn' comes from the following image of the Magic Square of **Saturn** by tracing in one continuous line the numbers starting from 1 and ending at 9:

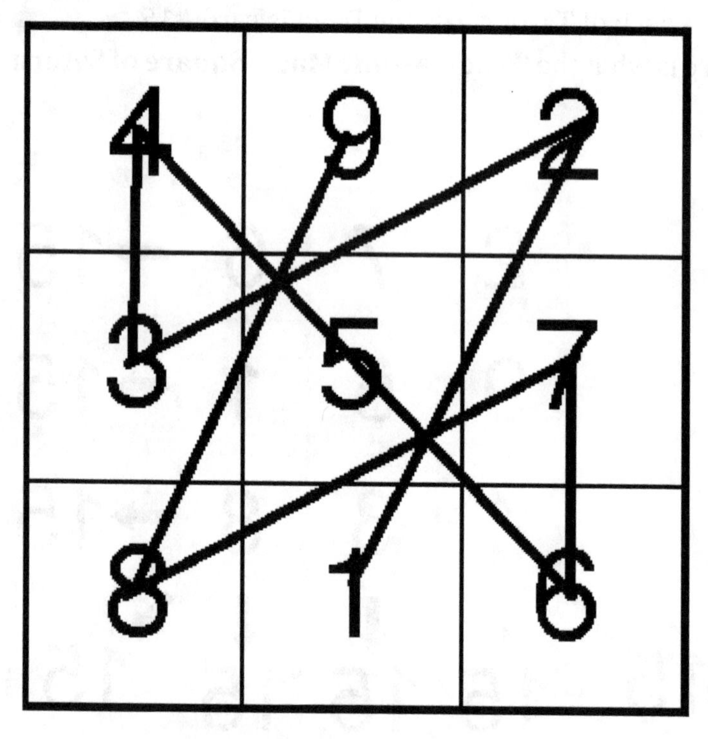

When displayed by itself as the Sigil of Saturn or the occult sign for Azazel, it is represented like this image below **or a variation of this very basic pattern of two 'X's next to each other**, such as the one on the cover of this book:

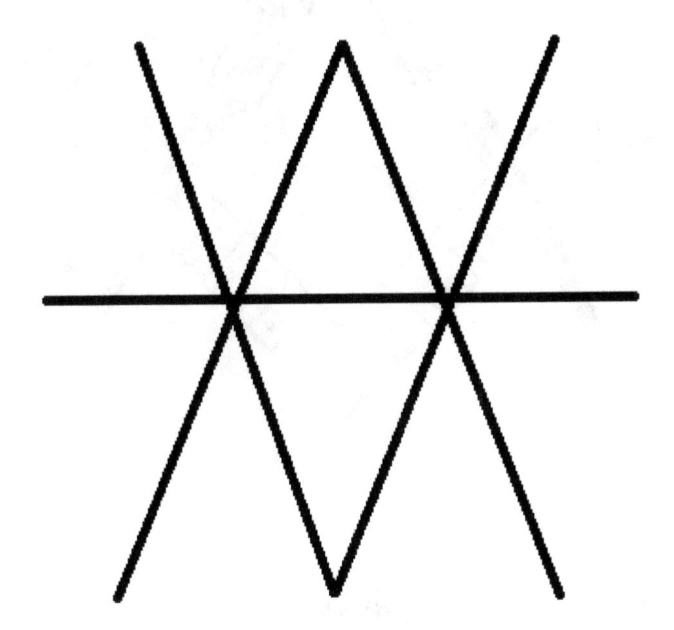

Since Saturn (Satan) is the god of the (upper echelon/Satanic) Freemasons, this explains the true origin of the Freemason's symbol of the square and compass. In its simplest form, the Sigil of Saturn is just two 'X's placed next to each other and here below represented by the square and compass.

Notice how the 'square' part of the Freemason's symbol nearly always has the ends broken off so as not to extend out and further risk betraying the true origination of their logo. Imagine the look of it with the square ends lengthening to match the distance of the compass arms. It would form 2 'X's next to each other. This is surely a representation of the Sigil of Saturn, the sign of their god, at least at the 33rd level of degree:

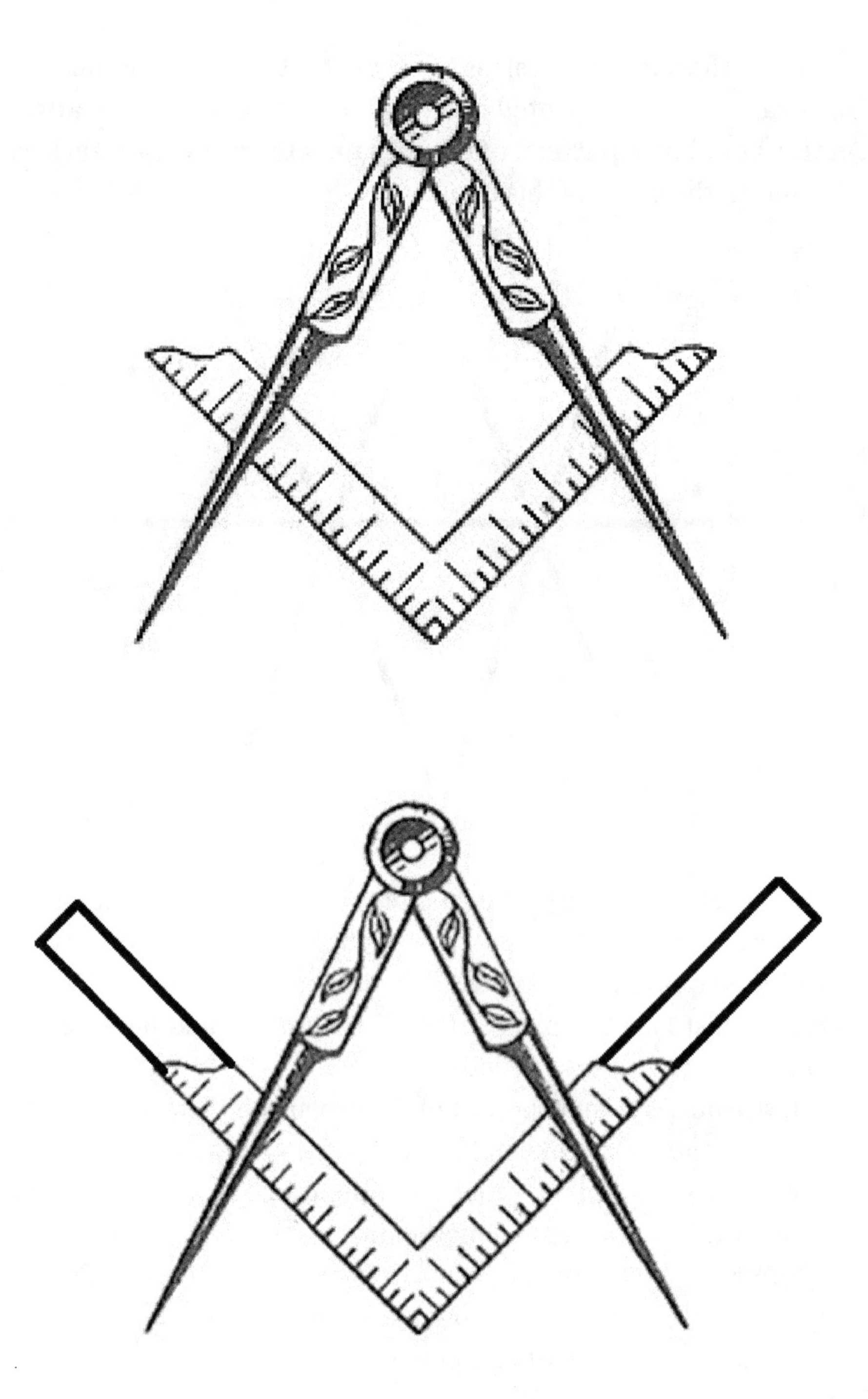

You get the idea though. Very basic, 2 'X's next to each other to the occultists equates to the Sigil of Saturn, known to you now as exactly a symbol of Satan.

The 'XX' theme is also used covertly to honor the god of time, Saturn, by placing virtually every watch/clock you'll ever see in an advertisement to 10:10, which in Roman numerals is XX.

There is even a double meaning here with the square and compass symbol I can show you behind the tools they specifically chose to be in their emblem. The square is used to make a square/cube that represents our 3D-physical world. The compass is used to make a circle, representative of the non-physical world, which encompasses all kinds of non-physical things like time, the supernatural and spirituality. The symbol of the square and compass represents everything in our plane of reality, and that Saturn is the god of that reality. Again, nothing here we aren't told in the Bible, right friend?

The Sigil of Saturn is also displayed in the Rockefeller family's crown jewel, the company currently (2015) the **#2** most valuable company in the entire world behind Apple Computer and that is E**XX**ON.

Now, all of this still doesn't explain the hexagram as a representation of Saturn, so let's get to that.

It is probable that the hexagram is based upon the hexagonal storm that is on Saturn, and that would make the most sense because it is a physical reality and the odds of a gigantic hexagon being visible on the planet Saturn specifically are remote at best.

It is my best guess that the hexagram is meant to be a representation of the hexagon on Saturn with 'rays' emanating out from it because Saturn is in fact a sun and is known to the occultists as the 'Black Sun'.

The 'black sun' moniker means that the brown dwarf sun called Saturn only puts out esoteric 'light' and is black to the unknowing masses. The Nazis used the 'black sun' symbol in their occult circles and something called the 'black sun' was an occult symbol hundreds and even thousands of years before the Nazis laid claim to it. Lots of homework for you to be sure on the topic of 'Saturn worship'.

The main point to take away is to know that the hexagram was originally used in occult ceremonies as an exact representation of the planet Saturn, to be used specifically in Saturn worship, which is Satan worship.

I told you that a 3D cube and in particular a **black** cube is also a symbol for the god Saturn, as black is also the sacred color for Saturn worship. To the occultists worshipping Saturn, the cube in general is a representation of our 3D world/physical sphere of consciousness, and a black cube is a representation of Saturn/ Satan himself, the god of this 3D world.

In the UN meditation room, the one that is supposed to be acceptable to **all** religious beliefs, there stands a black cube in the middle of the room. This is because virtually **all** religions/ mythologies are based on worshipping Saturn/Satan and always have been.

The Kaaba (English translation = cube) is the giant **black, cube-shaped building in Mecca, Saudi Arabia, and is the most sacred site in all of Islam.** This giant black cube has a mosque built around it, the Masjid al-Haram. **All Muslims around the world are required to face the Kaaba *specifically* during prayers, no matter where they are on the face of the Earth.**

The Muslims march around the giant black cube counterclockwise, exactly like the clouds revolving around the hexagonal storm system on Saturn, with the Kaaba of course precisely a 3D representation of Saturn.

Let's talk about the astrological sign for Saturn now and let's couple that with alchemy, also called 'Hermetic alchemy' from the god Hermes who is another representation of Saturn remember.

Here is what the ancient astrological sign of Saturn looks like:

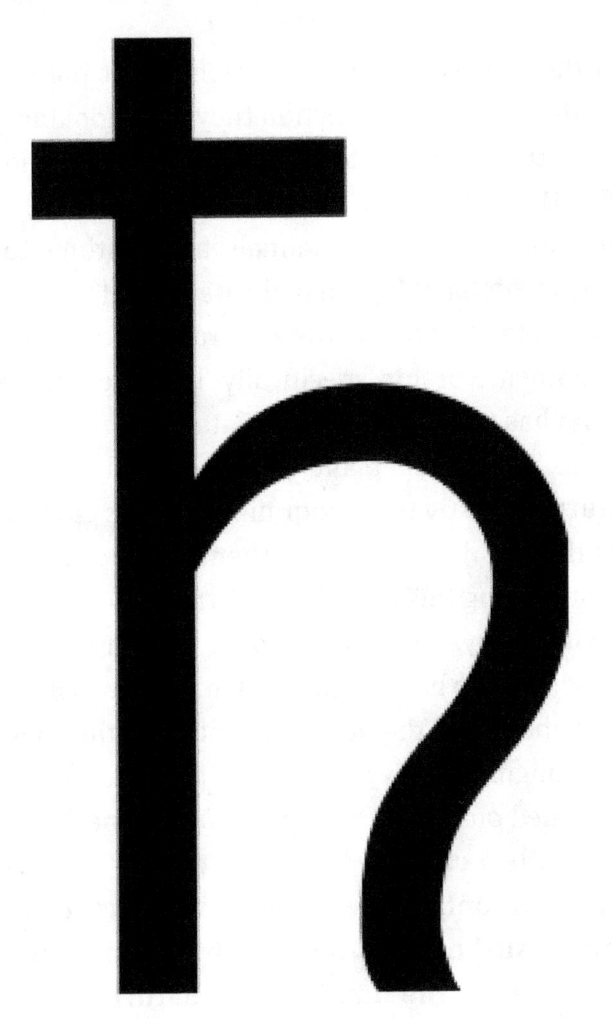

The astrological sign for Saturn is a cross/T/t and a sickle/H/h.

The sickle, if you'll remember from a little earlier, is what Cronus/Father Time/Death wields, so that is a direct representation of him. The cross above is arguably another display of Satan wielding the Babylonian Mystery Religion and King Nimrod/The Antichrist in particular.

The astrological sign of Saturn also doubles as the symbol for lead in alchemy. back in the day alchemy/science and the occult were one as the occult needed to advance science above all to fulfill the Great Plan of man turning into an immortal. The occultists had to be right there working with the scientists at the time guiding them along the path in the direction they were looking to go.

Lead is Saturn's associated metal in alchemy and ss it any wonder that the bullets that have killed hundreds of millions of humans and untold billions of animals, and continue to kill today are made of *lead*, Satan's own dedicated metal?

Since we're talking about the natural world here and things to do with Saturn worship specifically, let's see what else in the natural realm has to do with Saturn/Satan.......

Holly was the sacred plant of **Saturn** and was used at the Roman Saturnalia festival to honor him. Romans gave one another **holly wreaths** and decorated with them to honor the god Saturn. People are still doing this today at Christmas and this shouldn't be a surprise since they have exactly to do with the real meaning of Christmas, which is to honor Nimrod, which in turn honors exactly Satan. Think about this the next time you hear the song 'Deck the Halls' (with boughs of holly).

In my learned *opinion*, **it was *probably* a small *holly* wreath, which is literally a circular 'crown of thorns' and would have been very commonly known about in Jesus' day, that was placed upon Jesus' head to further the blasphemy of his torture and murder at the hands of the Saturn worshippers of the time, the Jews and the Romans.**

Not only is holly associated with Saturn, but Holly***wood*** is the preferred material used to make magical wands and staves from antiquity, never mind being the namesake of Hollywood, California. ***'The magic of holly wood'*** **??????** Truth really is stranger than fiction my friend.

Holly is to **Saturn** what **laurel** is to **Apollo/Nimrod**. This is also why there is a **laurel** wreath in particular on the UN logo. Laurel is the plant associated with the Antichrist and the United Nations is exactly his one world government. It's all right out there in the open for those with eyes to see.

You may have heard of ***Holly*** wood's **'Saturn Awards'**, which is like the Oscars for the field of sci-fi, fantasy and horror films in TV and movies.

The book and movie series 'The Lord of the Rings' is a reference to Saturn, and the all-seeing eye of Sauron is quite obvious as to what it is supposed to be, the eye of Saturn. If you look into it more closely, and I have, there is an aura to do with the Bible/New World Order that was going through J.R.R. Tolkien's mind when he crafted that series of books.

The 'Death Star' from Star Wars looks **exactly** like Saturn's moon Mimas:

And while we're on Star Wars, that movie is filled with occult-Saturn imagery if you know what to look for. George Lucas and/

or his 'handlers' are very knowledgeable about the occult. If you look up the various Star Wars symbols of both the rebel alliance and the Empire, you'll instantly see that the Empire is represented by Saturn symbology, including a cube, a 6-sided shape and even a cube that you will see now that you're awake to this. I would show them here but I don't have the means to secure the rights to do so. 'Google image' and you will see.

Some people say that the term 'Jedi' from Star Wars is talking about the Annunaki of the Sumerian mythology. At least I've come across that belief in my studies on this in particular. The 'Jedi Knights' are considered to be human wizards/warriors in touch with the 'Force', which in the Star Wars films is a combination of God and Satan. This is what the proponents of the New World Order believe and worship also: both God ***and*** Satan at the same time, and their view of God is represented exactly by 'the Force'.

The term 'Jedi' I would say comes from the Hebrew '**Jedi**diah', or 'Jedi' for short, and is the Holy name given to the wizard/warrior **King Solomon** when he was born. He would have been considered to be a mighty warrior because his father, King David, was one of the mightiest warriors of all time, slaying the Rephaim-giant Goliath with just a sling and a rock:

> *"....and sent word through Nathan the prophet, and he named him Jedidiah for the LORD'S sake."*
> *-2 Samuel 12:25*

The name 'Jedidiah' translated to English means 'friend/beloved of God'. So a Jedi in Star Wars-land is 'beloved of the Force' and is able to use the Force (God's) power for good, whereas the Empire consisting of Darth Vader, etc. uses the power of the Force for evil, the 'dark side' of the Force. This has to do with the subject of 'duality', everything having an opposite for balance in our world.

You're going to see at the end of this chapter the truth about King Solomon and why he is so revered and so important to the occultists and especially the Saturn-worshippers who run the New World Order today, and also why he is revered by the Freemasons in particular. There is a reason why King Solomon has been referred to as 'the greatest wizard of all time', and it's because he was the most effective conduit of Satan into our world since King Nimrod. That's why the Seal of Solomon is exactly the hexagram: It represents Saturn, who is Satan himself.

Hollywood is not the only modern day association with Saturn. Saturn symbology and influence is replete throughout our world and you have been seeing it your entire life and probably didn't even know it. I sure didn't until I started looking into these things with eyes to see.

In my first book I talked about the Apollo space program to get us to the moon.

With the wisdom gained through the research for this book I saw the connection that it was exactly the ***power*** of the ***Saturn*** rocket that propelled the ***Apollo*** space mission to the moon. It is going to be the **power** of **Satan** who propels the **Antichrist** to be the first immortal of the Great Plan. The Moon landings were arguably the apex of the example of how far man has progressed on his way to godhood on earth, only to be surpassed by bringing Nimrod back to life.

This was the ultimate occult commercial, and knowing what we do about how our world really operates, that's probably all it really was: A scripted commercial for the Satanists that control the world and how they get to do whatever they want to manipulate us into believing what they want us to believe.

The glaring inconsistencies when analyzing the moon landing documents, footage and photographs have been closely scrutinized by others searching for real truth and I would say the odds are better than not that we never made it past the upper atmosphere because of a huge list of bullet points I could go into. The film director Stanley Kubrick was alleged by some to have been the one who filmed the 'faked' Moon landings, putting clues to what he knew about the Great Plan in his movies. Just Google it and there is a story there with legs, I've already looked into it.

We probably never made it to the Moon and that is my honest opinion as of right now. This is not a far-fetched 'conspiracy theory' either. I could write a book about NASA in general, it was rotten from the start. Remember Operation Paperclip? NAZIS??? Yes, of course they are controlling everything, including our reality, because their god is the god of our reality through being the god of this world.

This revelation about the Moon landings should come as no surprise, as these are the exact same people who brought us the **'9/11 reality show'**. Right? Right, friend.

Staying on task here with Saturn symbology, in palm reading, which is a form of black magic, your middle finger is designated your **'Saturn'** finger.

I couldn't find the following anywhere, so it should be considered purely my opinion (as the rest of this book of course), but ***'flipping someone off'*** is showing them exactly the 'finger of Saturn'. To the occultists this is arguably effectively wishing/sending a curse right from Satan himself at someone. You are hexing them with a curse, and the term 'hex' comes from one of the exact original symbols of Satan, the hexagram, remember? You are literally showing them a symbol of Satan in the occultists' world. This is why it is so offensive to the person the hex is aimed at if the person sending the bad vibes is really intending provocation and harm when flipping them off. How many fights were started with someone flipping someone off? Countless.

One last symbol of Saturn, among thousands, that have made its way into our world, and this is one of the biggest ones, one of the most significant. I could not find this anywhere, and this is certainly my own interpretation, but it sure looks like the astrological/alchemical symbol of Saturn was also incorporated into the universal symbol of Communism via the hammer and sickle.

This should come as no surprise, since the founders of Communism were Satanists themselves and were only honoring their god, Saturn.

The two parts of the symbol of Saturn are the cross/T/t/ and the sickle/H/h. The sickle part is patently obvious (Saturn), and the hammer is meant to be the T/cross to the sickle, giving us the two parts to create the exact astrological representation of Saturn. The 'T' cross, also called the 'Tau' cross, and is representative particularly of Nimrod reincarnated as **Tammuz** the 'savior' god from the BMR. The symbol of Communism is exactly the sign of Saturn, so the symbol of Communism is also, therefore, a symbol of Satan.

And what is on the flag of the resurrected state of Israel today? The ancient symbol of Saturn, the hexagram.

If you start to look around with eyes to see, Satan is coming right out into the open now.

People are openly worshipping Satan and it is accepted by society to the same degree as any other religion. Nobody even gives it a second thought these days. The deception is nearly complete; we are certainly close to the End at this point.

To summarize, Saturn symbolism is exactly Satan symbolism. They are the exact same personality, the same being. Azazel, Cronus, etc. all the same. We're literally surrounded by his symbols, letting us constantly and subliminally know he is the god of this world and his people are in charge. He is so powerful it's off the human-comprehension scale. Off the chart powerful. And off the rails too, look at what he did before the Flood, and now soon to be again off the rails heading into the End until God will have had enough and bring an end to the game called 'The Fall of Man'.

We're not done yet here either. I'm going to show you even more how Satan is in control of things through the shared Abrahamic faith.

But first we've got some business to attend to with the Freemasons.......

Chapter 6/C

FREEMASONRY

We've already gone over the Freemason's symbol of the square and compass and how it's based on the **Sigil of Saturn**, of course ***it*** being taken directly from the ***'Magic*** **Square of *Saturn'***.

The compass and square that makes up the official Freemason symbol represents yet another hidden, esoteric meaning as we already went over, of the basic sacred geometric symbols those two tools are used to create: the circle and square. The circle represents that which is not physical but in our world, which is time/spirit/supernatural, with the square representing the physical, the cube, everything in the 3D world.

It is also a human being that is represented by the overlapping square and compass, because that's what we are: physical beings that will die and go back to dust and be recycled and contained in the physical world, coupled with supernatural/interdimensional eternal souls. We are part natural and part supernatural, just like the sign of the square and compass.

The commonly used symbol of the all-seeing eye, or as the Freemasons call it the 'Eye of Providence', is a complete deception with the public thinking it's meant to represent God our Heavenly Father. Most Freemasons believe this also, remember. Most of them don't have a clue about this Satanic business going on up at the 33rd level of degree and above. The exoteric meaning, the one given to the general public, is that it's God the Most High, but the

esoteric meaning among the true Satanists is that it's really their god ***Saturn.***

When I'm saying 'true Satanists' I mean the one's really running the show for Satan, the Illuminati. I'm not talking about Satanism 'lite' like the Church of Satan. Most people don't know that the Church of Satan is actually an **atheist** organization and they are just playing make-believe Satanists, although it appears Anton LaVey was working for 'them'. An image of him taken many years ago shows him wearing a ring with a giant black cube on it.

There is another possible esoteric meaning of the all-seeing eye that was added in ancient Egypt we need to go over to cover all our bases.

The Freemasons hold all things ancient Egyptian in very high accord and it is because they once ran the Great Plan. The Freemasons also have a high opinion of the Knights Templar, and it is because they once ran the Great Plan. King Solomon and the ancient Israelis are held in high regard by the Freemasons, and it is because they too once ran the Great Plan. Let's not forget that ancient Babylon and King Nimrod are held in high regard. Remember the Masonic 'Oath of Nimrod' from my first book, right? And so on and so forth. It is the symbols these people created and passed down the line to the people running the Great Plan that are with us today. Nearly if not all of them can be found within modern day Freemasonic imagery.

I have come across opinions that the all-seeing eye to the occultists ***also*** represents the pineal gland in humans, located at the front of the head nestled into the brain. The particular way the Egyptians drew it as the Eye of Horus has been said by some, and I can see this, that the Egyptian all-seeing eye design was based on what the human pineal gland and the other important physical parts to do with it looks like when situated in your body. Like if you were to cut someone open and look at how it's laid out, which they probably did. But that they knew the significance of this gland is interesting if this is the case.

The pineal gland up close looks like a tiny pinecone, and what is all over ancient Sumerian/Babylonian art? The gods are shown holding pinecones, and the pineal gland is widely believed in occult circles to be the seat of the soul. I would tend to agree with that also.

Onward we go with this quote from Albert Pike:

> *"You will hear shortly of the Rough ASHLAR and the Perfect ASHLAR, as part of the jewels of the Lodge. The rough Ashlar is said to be "a stone, as taken from the quarry, in its rude and natural state." The perfect Ashlar is said to be "a stone made ready by the hands of the workmen, to be adjusted by the working-tools of the Fellow-Craft." We shall not repeat the explanations of these symbols given by the York Rite. You may read them in its printed monitors. They are declared to allude to the self-improvement of the individual craftsman,--a continuation of the same superficial interpretation. The rough Ashlar is the PEOPLE, as a mass, rude and unorganized. The perfect Ashlar, or cubical stone, symbol of perfection, is the STATE, the rulers deriving their powers from the consent of the governed; the constitution and laws speaking the will of the people; the government harmonious, symmetrical, efficient, --its powers properly distributed and duly adjusted in equilibrium."*
>
> *-33rd degree Freemason Albert Pike, from his book Morals and Dogma*

Within every Freemasonry lodge are two stones as described above, with meanings exactly as detailed above. The symbol of perfection is manifested in their god Satan, represented to the occultists as a cube, with the Satanic **'rulers deriving their powers from the consent of the governed'**. Even though the people continuously vote for the lesser of two evils, they are still voting for evil. This could also be applied to how the Federal Reserve got into place, having been voted for by the 'rulers' named above.

Small black cubes are also used in ceremonies inside the lodge. With the images of the all-seeing eye, cubes, hexagrams and of course the square and compass, you are literally surrounded by images of Satan when standing in a Masonic lodge. This is pretty standard though, because we're constantly surrounded by Satanic symbolism in our everyday lives in society.

Something else to do with the Freemasons and Satan is their projection of duality. The floors of Masonic lodges are typically black and white checkerboards, and this is exactly to represent their view on God, or at least the Great Plan part of Freemasonry. They don't believe you can have one thing without the exact opposite of it to contrast or counterbalance it. There can be no up without down. No light without dark. No good without evil. It is exactly the position of the people running the New World Order today that evil needs to exist in our world to counterbalance the good, in order to test our souls.

This is how they think, and I understand this concept and will try to explain it to you now. It's not a good or a bad thing, it's just a thing, and it just is what it is. Everyone has their roles to play in this Divine Plan that is going on.

God ***needs*** 'evil' to test us. He needs things to go sideways on us to test our resolve, our mettle, our faith in Him that everything will be just fine in the end. If everything was going fine all the time while we were here there would be no testing us as humans. It would be boring and pointless to all parties involved. So instead of that, we all participate in the Divine Plan and the game called 'The Fall of Man'. In this game God is the Good Guy, Satan is the bad guy. We are the good guys on Earth for Team God, the brethren in Jesus Christ, and the job of being the bad guys is filled by Satan's followers. Everyone else is just 'here', stuck in the middle.

Satan had a purpose to start with, he just took it too far in the pre-Flood world. He was having too much fun turning the world on its ear, creating as much chaos to test us as possible and even too much chaos for God to accept. Satan overstepped his bounds through DNA meddling, especially by fathering the Nephilim. He's still doing the job he was tasked with, just from the confines of another dimension.

The image of **Baphomet**, if you look it up on an image search, is a complete dedication to this duality of evil needing to be manifested in the world to offset the good. The Satanic image has the breasts of a woman with an erect rod wrapped in serpents in place of his penis, representing the male-female duality. He is holding his hands, one towards the heavens and one towards the Earth in the so-called 'as above, so below' pose, representing the duality of Heaven and Earth. The image has other duality identifiers you can look into, but that is exactly what it's all about at the core.

What the image is relaying, especially to the evil ones, is that evil is necessary in the world, God acknowledges this, and whoever is running the Great Plan will be the ones filling that need.... with no regrets or shame about it. These are the leaders of the left hand path, with of course the saved brethren of Jesus representing the right hand path. By Jesus' own definition, if you are not saved of Him you are residing on the left hand path. This includes everyone in existence but the saved brethren.

The concept of 'duality' is how the evil ones justify the ghastly ceremonies they can stomach of sexually torturing and murdering other humans and especially babies and little kids. Drinking their blood. Stuff that you and I just can't even imagine taking part in but the people at the top actually look forward to these gruesome ceremonies. It also has to do with demonic possession and letting the dead Nephilim spirits participate in the Satanic bloodletting, including King Nimrod's spirit.

In the tradition of the ancient Satanists the Freemasons also use the image of the hexagram, as you should know by now, and they also use the image of the pentagram. I have not found for sure the origin of the pentagram and specifically who it is assigned to, but it is often associated with Satan. We're not going to go into the pentagram here, but I currently lean towards it probably representing Nimrod, the Antichrist. Remember all our 'holidays' are based on Nimrod, and the system he organized rules our world today, so it would make sense that he had his own 'star' if you will.

One thing I do want to tell you about to do with about Nimrod/ the Antichrist, since I learned what I did for this book, is that I believe that the number of the beast (Nimrod) from Revelation, **666**, comes from those pesky magic squares that I just told you about. Looking into this beyond my words here you will find this theory holds water and others have said the same thing before me.

Just as Azazel/Satan is associated with the ~~planet~~ **sun** Saturn, Nimrod is associated with the Sun itself as the first Sun god of the Babylonian Mystery Religion, and then is recycled as the Sun god on down the line from ancient Babylon, but not before Nimrod's Babylon in Sumer mind you.

There exists 'magic squares' for every planet/sun/moon they could see in ancient days, plus one to represent the Sun. This **'Magic Square of the Sun'** in my opinion, is the one that came to represent Nimrod as the 'Freemasonic Magic Square of Saturn' represents Saturn/Azazel/Satan.

If you add up all the numbers on the **'Magic square of the Sun'** you get exactly **666**, which by the nature of its origination is a ***magic number***, coming from a ***magic square***, that is used in real-life black magic. The 'Magic square of the Sun' itself is an occult tool, and the total of its numbers equals 666. 666 = the Magic Square of the Sun = King Nimrod deified as the Sun = the Antichrist = the beast. This is what I believe to be the true source of the number of the beast.

Jesus in Revelation, and throughout the Bible, gives us the clues we need to connect the dots and learn who the Antichrist is and what it's all about, but truly only for those with eyes to see.

Chapter 6/D

CHRISTIANITY

We're talking about some hard truths in this book, ugly truths. Truths that will temper our faith as long as you are able to keep everything in context, knowing we live in the Satanic Matrix, constantly under test.

Know for sure going into this chapter that I love the brethren in Jesus with all my heart and soul, and the last thing I'd ever want to do is hurt you or anyone else, but we've got to acknowledge that the evil ones have infiltrated our faith from the start. This chapter is certainly not intended at all to damage your faith, but to scale off some of the occult elements that have crept in so you can know the real truth and then do your own research so you can make whatever decisions about that you're going to.

We live in an intentionally bizarre-backwards world where we are ruled by the most evil people on the planet and the deception they help to keep going keeps them perpetually in power. For them to accomplish this, they need to control the most important aspects of society, which is exactly religion, politics and the economy, all of which they control today as they have forever.

They have infiltrated everything, including our precious faith as followers of Jesus Christ. What is Christianity today is nothing like He meant to be. I think this is why Jesus has shown me so much truth, because I want to know the truth in order to leverage it into exactly what God ideally wants from us: 100% respect and adoration. This can only come about by knowing the real truth so you can separate yourself from the truly Satanic influence; there is no other way to put it.

So. Let's look at the Saturn symbology specifically within the Catholic Church, because that is the avenue upon which the true teachings of Jesus were hijacked not long after their inception.

To start with, the color black seems to be the official color of the Catholic Church. The priests wear black. The nuns wear black. Black is the official color of Saturn remember. The color white is represented in the Bible as being the Holy color, not black. Why aren't they wearing white? It is because they are honoring the god Saturn, either knowingly (upper echelon) or unknowingly (the practicing Catholic masses).

Most people, most CATHOLICS, have never heard of something called the 'Black Pope'. You see, there are actually **two** Popes running the Catholic Church from Rome. One is the public face of Catholicism, the exoteric version, the 'white' Pope, and one is the occult version, the esoteric version, the **Black** Pope. The regular Pope is symbolic of the Sun worship (Nimrod/Antichrist) within the Catholic Church, while the Black Pope is symbolic of Saturn/ Black Sun (Satan) worship. The Black Pope is also **the official head of the Jesuits**, who you learned about in the first book, and the symbol of the Jesuits to this day is right below:

As you can see, the symbols in the center are surrounded by **specifically** the Sun. This is a representation of, again, King Nimrod.

Do you see the cross standing on top of the 'H' that is stamped in the middle of the Sun? This is an esoteric version of the astrological sign of Saturn, the cross (T or t) atop of the sickle (H or h), so there are two Satanic symbols contained in this one symbol, and we're not done yet.

The letters 'IHS', when used together and all-capitalized, exactly like in the Jesuit symbol, originally was the sacred monogram of the Roman god Bacchus, who is the same thing as the Greek god Dionysus. Both Bacchus and Dionysus had their birthdays on **December 25** and both are just more representations of exactly King Nimrod. Bacchus is also often represented in ancient art with a head band covered with **crosses**. The symbol of the Jesuits is nothing but Satan/Nimrod worship merged together.

Here's something for you, these are rings the Jesuits used to wear in the 1600s. We know this because hundreds of these were found in the shipwreck of the La Belle, which went down in 1684:

There is also something to do with what is on those rings, which is the Sigil of Saturn flanked by two pillars, which is also exactly '9-11' in Roman numerals. This probably has to do with the Twin Towers and 9/11. I've ventured this avenue of research a little and appears there is something there, but I'll leave that for you to look into.

I've seen plenty of images of the Pope wearing **hexagrams** on his hat, all representative of Saturn of course. **Why are there symbols of Satan on the hat of supposedly the most holy man on the planet?** Because the entire Roman Catholic system is mired in a Satanic deception. These images of hexagrams on the hat of the pope are currently available with a simple internet search of 'pope hat hexagram'.

In fact, let's briefly discuss the different hats the Pope wears. Let's start with his ***Saturn Hat***. Yes, the Pope has a hat called a Saturn Hat he wears for special (Satanic) occasions.

Another hat the Pope wears, called a 'mitre hat', is meant to represent the hats the ancient priests of Dagon wore, with Dagon of course another representation of Satan. Google search is your friend for now, but might not be in the future so use it to help fill your mind with confirmed facts.

Hopefully by now you can truly see what Saturn worship really equates to, it is the ancient exoteric version of esoteric Satan worship, and it has been in our midst for thousands of years, and it is among us here today.

By small groups of people coveting the Satan worship to themselves so they can reap rewards in this life instead of the next, they have passed this Great Plan down the Satanic family line for thousands of years since Nimrod.

Chapter 6/E

JUDAISM

"And Stephen, full of grace and power, was performing great wonders and signs among the people. But some men from what was called the Synagogue of the Freedmen, including both Cyrenians and Alexandrians, and some from Cilicia and Asia, rose up and argued with Stephen. But they were unable to cope with the wisdom and the Spirit with which he was speaking. Then they secretly induced men to say, "We have heard him speak blasphemous words against Moses and against God." And they stirred up the people, the elders and the scribes, and they came up to him and dragged him away and brought him before the Council. They put forward false witnesses who said, "This man incessantly speaks against this holy place and the Law; for we have heard him say that this Nazarene, Jesus, will destroy this place and alter the customs which Moses handed down to us." And fixing their gaze on him, all who were sitting in the Council saw his face like the face of an angel."

-Acts 6:8-15

"You also took along the tabernacle of Moloch (Nimrod/ Antichrist) and the star of the god Rompha (Saturn/Satan), the images which you made to worship. I also will remove you beyond Babylon."

-Acts 7:42, words of Stephen to the Judaic authorities

"Now when they heard this, they were cut to the quick, and they began gnashing their teeth at him. But being full of the Holy Spirit, he gazed intently into heaven and saw the glory of God, and Jesus standing at the right hand of God; and he said, "Behold, I see the heavens opened up and the Son of Man standing at the right hand of God." But they cried out with a loud voice, and covered their ears and rushed at him with one impulse. When they had driven him out of the city, they began stoning him; and the witnesses laid aside their robes at the feet of a young man named Saul. They went on stoning Stephen as he called on the Lord and said, "Lord Jesus, receive my spirit!" Then falling on his knees, he cried out with a loud voice, "Lord, do not hold this sin against them!" Having said this, he fell asleep."

-Acts 7:54-60

The quotes directly above from the New Testament, Acts of the Apostles, have to do with a man named Stephen who is traditionally regarded as the first martyr of Christianity. That is, he held onto his faith in Jesus Christ even as he was being brutally executed for it. At his trial where he was accused of blasphemy for preaching the Gospel as a follower of Jesus, he denounced the Judaic authorities who condemned him to death by stoning. The condemned man Stephen was flat calling them out, accusing them of exactly Satan/Antichrist worship.

Stephen's execution was witnessed by 'a young man named Saul', who would go on to persecute the early Christian church. Later on in life, Saul saw the light and found Jesus, or Jesus found him it seems, turning into who we now know as Paul the apostle. Paul as you know is the author of many books of the New Testament.

I've tried to gauge current-day Judaism's position on Saturn/Satan by Googling exactly this and reading everything I could find to get a consensus that I felt would stand up to scrutiny by all.

I agree with some things and not others that Judaism professes to believe about God and Satan, and we'll get to that. First I want to give a summary of what it appears that Judaism in general believes about Satan according to what I've read at various pro-Judaic websites, and I'll just put it in as basic of a statement as possible:

The view of Satan by Judaism is radically different than that of mainstream Christianity. Judaism believes that angels do not have free will and therefore cannot sin. Thereby, Satan is not a fallen angel; he is actually working for God as our supreme tester. The Book of Job is cited by Judaism in general as the go-to source for the best representation of who and what Satan is. The idea that Satan is against God equates to polytheism, giving Satan god-like status for being powerful enough to oppose God. This view is unacceptable to the Judaic version of the monotheistic/Abrahamic faith. Satan, as an agent of God, is also a representation of God as the evil that is necessary to test our souls while we're here. Satan has to have permission from God to be able to interact with us on Earth to test us. Therefore, if God knows all, He knows that Satan is using his followers to fulfill Biblical prophecy with God's blessing, even though they are committing great evil in the process. The verses from Deuteronomy 30:15 and Isaiah 45:7 are cited often to reinforce this position, with both verses stating that ***God is one entity, indivisible, maker of everything including good and evil.*** *A minority of Judaism are calling Satan a metaphor for the 'Evil Inclination', where it seems the majority believe that Satan is a real being and equate Satan the supernatural being as our supreme tester/ adversary.*

We're back into our very real concept that the people running the world believe, and that in one word is called **duality**. There has to be evil to oppose the good in order to not only create an environment to test mankind, to test our souls, but to have balance in our 3D world. This is exactly related to the dualism prominently displayed in both the occult and in Freemasonry also. Good and Bad. Black and white. Ying and Yang. As above, so below, etc. The black and white checkerboard floors in the Masonic lodges, the Baphomet imagery showing the duality they live by, etc.

It is Judaism's position that the Christian's believe that God would never intentionally create an evil entity like Satan, and that he rebelled of his own accord and was a fallen angel.

The real truth, in my opinion, lies somewhere in the middle of what both Christians and Jews believe.

Satan **did** rebel prior to the Flood and got in big trouble for overstepping his bounds, but he was still retained by God to do the job he created Satan for, which is to be the god of this world **and** our divine tester until God says it's time to hand it off to Jesus to rule the Millennial Kingdom.

During my research trying to pin down the Judaic view of Satan I also came across something that reaffirms what I said earlier in this book about the entity called 'Lucifer'. Nearly all references I found show the Jews believe the verse in Isaiah about Lucifer is actually about the King of Babylon, but seem to shy away from figuring/naming the king as Nimrod specifically.

Now, let's bring Hitler and his **black-cube moustache** into this discussion now that we are up to our eyeballs in this whole Saturn-worship agenda. Hitler was also involved with Saturn worship and this was partially his motivation to try and exterminate Judaism and take over the Synagogue of Satan's end of the Great Plan. I don't buy for a minute the excuse given by the historians as to why Hitler wore his moustache like he did. He wore it that way to display the sign of Saturn right on his face to the media and to all his followers. Displaying occult symbols helps attract occult power, which was exactly what Hitler was trying to do and certainly did.

We know from my first book that Hitler wasn't a Christian man at all and actually despised the saved brethren. Hitler was an occultist, a Satanist to be sure behind the scenes, but I had no idea he too was wrapped up in Saturn worship until I dug in for this book.

Hitler said a lot of derogatory things about the Jews during his climb to power except the most important, controversial and suppressed one of all: That elements of Judaism are engaged in Saturn worship and have been for thousands of years. The synagogue of ***Saturn.***

Hitler didn't bring up the Saturn worship within Judaism as part of his propaganda because he himself was fully engaged in Saturn worship, wanting to leave all of that esoteric business safely in the shadows because Saturn worship is exactly the religion of the people who run the planet for Satan.

Hitler wanted to be the kingpin of Saturn worship, which would equate to him being the modern day Antichrist, and he nearly made it. Since he certainly was not King Nimrod, however, it was destined for failure and did fail as part of the Divine Plan.

Remember, at the time of Hitler's reign of power the Nazis were aligned with Italy, who in turn, since the Vatican is in Italy, was aligned with the Vatican, the **other** branch of the Satanic New World Order/Great Plan. Hitler was looking to extinguish the Synagogue of ***Saturn*** branch of the Great Plan, then take the reins of the Catholic Church as the New World Order Antichrist. This was his goal ***in my opinion***.

The **ancient** image of the swastika, the one most associated with Hitler and the Nazi party......could it be a representation of Saturn? Some have said it is a Sun symbol, and being it's always black I would say a **black sun** symbol if anything, and that is of course Saturn.

I came across something else that to me seems just as, if not more, plausible, and that's the fact that you can make a swastika from the magic square of Saturn, both the masculine (left image below) and the feminine (right image below) representation of it. There's that pesky 'duality' again, male and female.

This possibly first originated from the Chinese/Asian version of the Magic Square of Saturn, called the **Lo Shu square**.

The symbol of the swastika has been used in Asian countries for thousands of years, and is prominently displayed in ancient art of all kinds. The swastika had to originate somewhere in the ancient world, and with what we know so far about how things went down in the ancient past regarding Satan's handiwork, this theory of the swastika's origination as a magical symbol of Saturn is the simplest, most obvious, and most probable in my opinion. All of the numbers even add the same along each line to 25, so it's perfectly balanced in other words, just like ***they*** like.

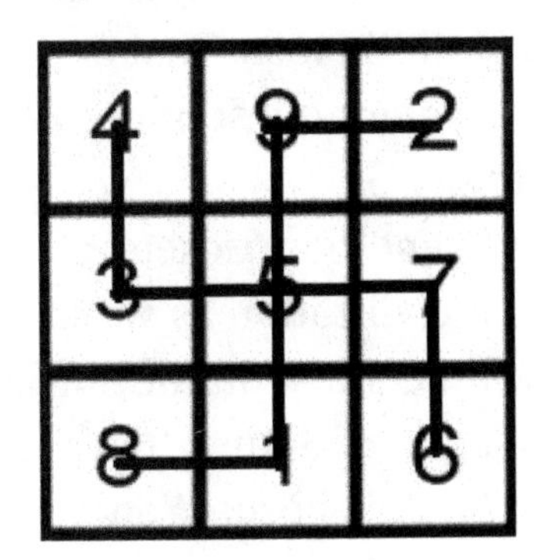

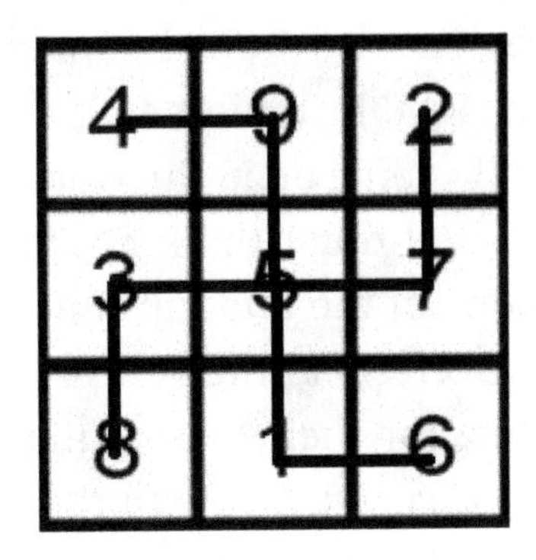

Hitler was getting money from the Synagogue of Saturn at the start but Hitler outgrew his chains, mutinied and turned on them, seeking to grab all the power for himself. This is exactly what happened with Napoleon: A charismatic leader was installed and financially backed with the intention of him being a puppet for the Satanists, but his power grew so great he rose up and mutinied against his puppeteers.

Remember, these are the backstabbing-est, most evil, ruthless, vile, untrustworthy and conniving people on the planet....even to each other. There is no loyalty within the ranks of the Great Plan.

Please keep in mind for sure that not all Jews, just like not all Christians or Freemasons, are involved in Saturn/Satan worship. In fact, it is a minority within these groups that are actual Satanists, with most people not having a clue as to what is really going on.

They just follow along with the herd like most people tend to do, never questioning what is truthfully going on in the world around them.

One of my best friends is a Messianic Jewish lady and I know for a fact she's not out worshipping Satan behind my back. We're talking about a small minority of people here, not 'John and Judy Jew' down the street for sure, not at all. Jews are inflicted with the same things we are by the NWO: vaccines, fluoride, aspartame. How some of the foods that are on the shelves today can be stamped 'Kosher' I have no idea because a lot of the ingredients weren't made by God but man, especially GMO foods. That doesn't seem right. Just another example of people not questioning what is really going on in the world around them.

Now, I don't think my Jewish lady friend has 'tickets' to get into one of the underground cities when civilization as we know it ends. Her and the rest of the Jews will be stuck on the surface fighting for their lives while the Synagogue of Saturn 'Jews' are safely tucked away with the rest of the Satanic horde. You better believe that every important operative of the NWO-infrastructure has clearance to get into the Deep Underground Military Bases, DUMBs, and their immediate families. That group of operatives is comprised of "Jews, Christians, Buddhists, Atheists, or 'whatever'".

So. The Saturn worship was paying off in spades for Hitler and the Nazis, and they were guided through their occult practices to creating unbelievably advanced technology for the time, including, I believe, anti-gravitational technology. If they would have finished their nuclear bomb first, the plans for which they had in motion, they would be ruling the world today with a Satanic one world government. It was not to be though. Not yet. This thing is going to go off by God's watch.....not Father Time's.

Hitler wasn't the only one who tried to relieve the Synagogue of Satan of their Saturn worship.....

Our Heavenly Father in the Old Testament through His prophets was not shy about chastising the ancient Israelites/Judahites for constantly falling back into Saturn worship to try and gain power and glory on Earth.

God reprimanding the ancient Israelites seems to take up quite a bit of space in the Old Testament if you honestly think about it. Moses, Isaiah, Ezekiel, Jeremiah, etc. spent a lot of their words calling out the nation of Israel as a whole to start with and then the Judahites down the road as straying from God, trying to play both sides of the coin: worship of God and Satan at the same time as if they are the same being but different facets. Satan is the 'lesser god' to God the Creator, our Heavenly Father. If you want the most financial success and power in this physical world, it is exactly the god of this world you worship, Satan.

"Did you present Me with sacrifices and grain offerings in the wilderness for forty years, O house of Israel? You also carried along Sikkuth your king and Kiyyun, your images, the star of your god which you made for yourselves. Therefore, I will make you go into exile beyond Damascus," says the Lord, whose name is the God of hosts."

-Amos 5:26-27 (Sikkuth translates to Molech/King Nimrod and Kiyyun translates to Saturn)

Do you understand the real meaning of the above quote? Right from the Holy Bible. Book of Amos. God Himself tells us that some of the Israelites were literally worshipping exactly ***Nimrod*** and ***Satan*** during their 40 years of wandering the wilderness after the Exodus from Egypt.

Every time they fell out of God's graces it's because they went exactly to Saturn/BMR worship, which equates to Satanism no matter how you slice it.

"The word of the Lord which came to Zephaniah son of Cushi, son of Gedaliah, son of Amariah, son of Hezekiah, in the days of Josiah son of Amon, king of Judah:

"I will completely remove all things From the face of the earth," declares the Lord.

"I will remove man and beast; I will remove the birds of the sky and the fish of the sea,

And the ruins along with the wicked; And I will cut off man from the face of the earth," declares the Lord.

"So I will stretch out My hand against Judah and against all the inhabitants of Jerusalem.

And I will cut off the remnant of Baal from this place, and the names of the idolatrous priests along with the priests.

"And those who bow down on the housetops to the host of heaven,

And those who bow down and swear to the Lord and yet swear by Milcom (Nimrod),

And those who have turned back from following the Lord,

And those who have not sought the Lord or inquired of Him."

-Zephaniah 1:1-6

'And those who bow down and swear to the Lord and yet swear by Milcom (Nimrod)'. In this verse from the above OT passage, God is calling out the ancient Judahites for worshipping both Nimrod and God at the same time. Worship of Nimrod to honor Satan exactly equates to worship of Jesus to honor God. This is why the Babylonian Mystery Religion is so important to understand as a counterpart to Saturn worship.

It is important and significant in my work here to show what Jesus had to say about the Jews worshipping Saturn during His time here on Earth.

To start with, Jesus was soundly rejected by the Saturn-worshipping Judaic authorities at the time He came because He was not their 'messiah'. Not at all. **King Nimrod** is. And when Nimrod is brought back to life he will fill that role for the Jews, Christians and Muslims, who are all unknowingly waiting for the

'Saturn messiah' whether they know it or not, who is exactly King Nimrod.

This is how complete the Satanic deception is, so thorough that even most Christians are unintentionally and unknowingly waiting for the Saturn messiah through the Catholic system and when he shows up they will be completely deceived, but you won't, friend.

The Pope, who is exactly a representative for Nimrod/ Antichrist, will tell the Catholics to accept the Antichrist as the returned "Jesus" because the Antichrist will be able to claim the Holidays, Cross, etc. as his own because they are!!

Hopefully at this point in your studies you see this won't be a hard thing to accomplish with society in general in a complete stupor about what's really going on. They are too busy watching American Idol or that Kardashian claptrap, playing video games, watching online porn.....whatever. Humanity in general are doing anything and everything **BUT** paying attention to what is really going on around them, and it was set up this way in order for the Satanic conspiracy to succeed.

Jesus Christ is the exact opposite of Saturn worship, the BMR and the Great Plan. You should easily understand now why the Roman Catholic Church has drug the name and reputation of God and Jesus through the mud for 2,000 years, which was **their job**.

When Jesus showed up in the flesh and started His ministry around the age of 30, He immediately started in on the Synagogue of Saturn. His confronting of the Judaic leaders at the time about their fallen status really rocked the boat. He probably scared the living daylights out of them because they knew exactly who He was. Jesus did not mince words at all when getting into these face-offs with the leaders of Judaism at the time. Although there are many confrontations in the New Testament, here are just two. Don't just skim over these for sure, it is very important to read every single verse and to let each line register in your mind what is being said:

"Then Jesus spoke to the crowds and to His disciples, saying: "The scribes and the Pharisees have seated themselves in the chair of Moses; therefore all that they tell you, do and observe, but do not do according to their deeds; for they say things and do not do them. They tie up heavy burdens and lay them on men's shoulders, but they themselves are unwilling to move them with so much as a finger.

*But they do all their deeds to be noticed by men; for they broaden their *****phylacteries***** and lengthen the tassels of their garments. They love the place of honor at banquets and the chief seats in the synagogues, and respectful greetings in the market places, and being called Rabbi by men.*

But do not be called Rabbi; for One is your Teacher, and you are all brothers. Do not call anyone on earth your father; for One is your Father, He who is in heaven. Do not be called leaders; for One is your Leader, that is, Christ. But the greatest among you shall be your servant. Whoever exalts himself shall be humbled; and whoever humbles himself shall be exalted.

"But woe to you, scribes and Pharisees, hypocrites, because you shut off the kingdom of heaven from people; for you do not enter in yourselves, nor do you allow those who are entering to go in. Woe to you, scribes and Pharisees, hypocrites, because you devour widows' houses, and for a pretense you make long prayers; therefore you will receive greater condemnation.

"Woe to you, scribes and Pharisees, hypocrites, because you travel around on sea and land to make one proselyte; and when he becomes one, you make him twice as much a son of hell as yourselves.

"Woe to you, blind guides, who say, 'Whoever swears by the temple, that is nothing; but whoever swears by the gold of the temple is obligated.' You fools and blind men! Which is more important, the gold or the temple that sanctified the

gold? And, 'Whoever swears by the altar, that is nothing, but whoever swears by the offering on it, he is obligated.' You blind men, which is more important, the offering, or the altar that sanctifies the offering? Therefore, whoever swears by the altar, swears both by the altar and by everything on it. And whoever swears by the temple, swears both by the temple and by Him who dwells within it. And whoever swears by heaven, swears both by the throne of God and by Him who sits upon it.

"Woe to you, scribes and Pharisees, hypocrites! For you tithe mint and dill and cumin, and have neglected the weightier provisions of the law: justice and mercy and faithfulness; but these are the things you should have done without neglecting the others. You blind guides, who strain out a gnat and swallow a camel!

"Woe to you, scribes and Pharisees, hypocrites! For you clean the outside of the cup and of the dish, but inside they are full of robbery and self-indulgence. You blind Pharisee, first clean the inside of the cup and of the dish, so that the outside of it may become clean also.

"Woe to you, scribes and Pharisees, hypocrites! For you are like whitewashed tombs which on the outside appear beautiful, but inside they are full of dead men's bones and all uncleanness. So you, too, outwardly appear righteous to men, but inwardly you are full of hypocrisy and lawlessness.

"Woe to you, scribes and Pharisees, hypocrites! For you build the tombs of the prophets and adorn the monuments of the righteous, and say, 'If we had been living in the days of our fathers, we would not have been partners with them in shedding the blood of the prophets.' So you testify against yourselves, that you are sons of those who murdered the prophets. Fill up, then, the measure of the guilt of your fathers. You serpents, you brood of vipers, how will you escape the sentence of hell?

"Therefore, behold, I am sending you prophets and wise men and scribes; some of them you will kill and crucify, and some of them you will scourge in your synagogues, and persecute from city to city, so that upon you may fall the guilt of all the righteous blood shed on earth, from the blood of righteous Abel to the blood of Zechariah, the son of Berechiah, whom you murdered between the temple and the altar. Truly I say to you, all these things will come upon this generation."

-Matthew 23:1-16

"So Jesus was saying to those Jews who had believed Him, "If you continue in My word, then you are truly disciples of Mine; and you will know the truth, and the truth will make you free." They answered Him, "We are Abraham's descendants and have never yet been enslaved to anyone; how is it that You say, 'You will become free'?"

Jesus answered them, "Truly, truly, I say to you, everyone who commits sin is the slave of sin. The slave does not remain in the house forever; the son does remain forever. So if the Son makes you free, you will be free indeed. I know that you are Abraham's descendants; yet you seek to kill Me, because My word has no place in you. I speak the things which I have seen with My Father; therefore you also do the things which you heard from your father."

They answered and said to Him, "Abraham is our father." Jesus said to them, "If you are Abraham's children, do the deeds of Abraham. But as it is, you are seeking to kill Me, a man who has told you the truth, which I heard from God; this Abraham did not do. You are doing the deeds of your father."

They said to Him, "We were not born of fornication; we have one Father: God."

Jesus said to them, "If God were your Father, you would love Me, for I proceeded forth and have come from God, for I have not even come on My own initiative, but He sent Me. Why do you not understand what I am saying? It is because you cannot hear My word. You are of your father the devil, and you want to do the desires of your father. He was a murderer from the beginning, and does not stand in the truth because there is no truth in him. Whenever he speaks a lie, he speaks from his own nature, for he is a liar and the father of lies. But because I speak the truth, you do not believe Me. Which one of you convicts Me of sin? If I speak truth, why do you not believe Me? He who is of God hears the words of God; for this reason you do not hear them, because you are not of God."

-John 8: 31-47

By the time you tally up all the facts of what is, it is hard to come to the conclusion that certain elements of Judaism ***aren't*** involved with Saturn worship for the very reasons I'm giving.

How about the use of 'tefillin' by Jewish males? What are 'tefillin' you're probably wondering?

Tefillin are two small ***black cubes***, representative exactly of the god Saturn, that contain 4 specific verses of scripture, 2 from Exodus and 2 from Deuteronomy. According to Jewish tradition, upon a Jewish boy's 13th birthday he is Bar Mitzvah and now required to participate in adult traditions, one of which is to wear the tefillin every morning for prayer. It is my understanding that most Jews today don't do this, maybe because they know what it really represents.

The first and most important of the verses contained in the cubes seems to be the verse from Deuteronomy below that I listed earlier, **because it contains the statement 'the Lord is one'.**

This refers to Satan being a facet or representative of the Most High God and therefore approves of worshipping him. 'The Lord is one' means God is everything, even evil in the form of Saturn/Satan.

Another reason this verse is the most important is that it contains the metaphorical language to physically wear the words from the verses. This is a Pharisee interpretation from what I've looked into. In the verse I gave three pages back from Matthew 23, the term **'phylacteries'** is used by Jesus. **Phylacteries are exactly tefillin, the black cubes of Saturn.**

According to the Pharisees, wearing tefillin was based upon biblical law, citing the following verse chiefly and three additional others to justify the existence and use of:

> *"Hear, O Israel! The Lord is our God, the Lord is one! You shall love the Lord your God with all your heart and with all your soul and with all your might. These words, which I am commanding you today, shall be on your heart. You shall teach them diligently to your sons and shall talk of them when you sit in your house and when you walk by the way and when you lie down and when you rise up. You shall bind them as a sign on your hand and they shall be as frontals on your forehead. You shall write them on the doorposts of your house and on your gates."*
>
> *-Deuteronomy 6:4-9*

Now let's talk about Kabballah, also called 'Jewish mysticism', which is a politically correct way to say 'black magic'.

You know what? I don't even need to elaborate on that here. The term 'Kabballah' says everything you need to know about it.

'Kabballah' is a composite of two words: Kabba (cube) and Allah (god). The term Kabballah literally means 'cube god'..... Saturn.....**Satan.**

Let's wrap this section up with my accounting of exactly what happened with the fall of King Solomon, one of God's greatest prophets.....and greatest heartbreaks.

Solomon was the son of the great King David, who was the slayer of the **Rephaim**-giant Goliath.

He was the author of the Old Testament books the Song of Solomon, Proverbs, and Ecclesiastes.

He was considered the wisest man in the Bible until Jesus' appearance.........and he was a Satan worshipper.

So how could Solomon be both a prophet of the Most High, getting his works into the Holy Bible, and also be a Saturn/Satan worshipper?

It goes back to that duality thing again. Evil is necessary in our world to execute our spiritual test, and this is the excuse Solomon used to justify to God his involvement with Saturn worship.

We're going to break down the following verse from 1 Kings because it tells us not only about Solomon, but why Judaism is still mired in Saturn worship today, even if a lot of Jews aren't aware of it, which I don't believe they are. The Synagogue of Satan, today represented by the Rothschild contingency, have largely co-opted the whole of Judaism through their money power, buying off the leadership and by default dragging the rest of Judaism in by default.

Judaism has bounced in and out of Satanic control since the days of King Solomon and before. A certain segment never let it go, the Synagogue of Saturn. That's exactly why the Pharisees were wearing tefillin when they were face-to-face with Jesus Christ 900 years after the reign of Solomon:

"Now King Solomon loved many foreign women along with the daughter of Pharaoh: Moabite, Ammonite, Edomite, Sidonian, and Hittite women, from the nations concerning which the Lord had said to the sons of Israel, "You shall not associate with them, nor shall they associate with you, for they will surely turn your heart away after their gods." Solomon held fast to these in love.

He had seven hundred wives, princesses, and three hundred concubines, and his wives turned his heart away. For when Solomon was old, his wives turned his heart away after other gods; and his heart was not wholly devoted to the Lord his God, as the heart of David his father had been.

For Solomon went after Ashtoreth the goddess of the Sidonians and after Milcom the detestable idol of the Ammonites. Solomon did what was evil in the sight of the Lord, and did not follow the Lord fully, as David his father had done.

Then Solomon built a high place for Chemosh the detestable idol of Moab, on the mountain which is east of Jerusalem, and for Molech the detestable idol of the sons of Ammon. Thus also he did for all his foreign wives, who burned incense and sacrificed to their gods.

Now the Lord was angry with Solomon because his heart was turned away from the Lord, the God of Israel, who had appeared to him twice, and had commanded him concerning this thing, that he should not go after other gods; but he did not observe what the Lord had commanded. So the Lord said to Solomon, "Because you have done this, and you have not kept My covenant and My statutes, which I have commanded you, I will surely tear the kingdom from you, and will give it to your servant. Nevertheless I will not do it in your days for the sake of your father David, but I will tear it out of the hand of your son. However, I will not tear away all the kingdom, but I will give one tribe to your son for the sake of My servant David and for the sake of Jerusalem which I have chosen."

-1 Kings 11:1-13

I'm going to now break this passage down completely according to my interpretation, so you can fully understand the meaning of this verse.

"Now King Solomon loved many foreign women along with the daughter of Pharaoh: Moabite, Ammonite, Edomite, Sidonian, and Hittite women, from the nations concerning which the Lord had said to the sons of Israel, "You shall not associate with them, nor shall they associate with you,

for they will surely turn your heart away after their gods." Solomon held fast to these in love.

Solomon broke the ice in going against God by ignoring His warnings and involving himself with women who came from Satanic-occult backgrounds after he was specifically ordered not to. They were all following Satan and the Babylonian Mystery Religion back in those days as today, all worshipping Satan in one form or another. As we just learned, that's all that exists in the mythologies to worship no matter what you call the 'gods', it's just Satan and Nimrod and to a lesser degree Semiramis/Ishtar/Astarte/etc.

Solomon got tripped up and fell in love with some of these women, and it's virtually a given that when in love and especially when getting sex, a man is a moldable lump of clay for a woman. Let alone a handful of beautiful women all at once wanting to be with King Solomon.

A man in this physical-euphoric state will forsake all in this world: family, friends....life in general, as long as he is getting sex, especially to the degree Solomon was.

You know how it goes and we've all experienced this: Your male buddy gets a new squeeze and you don't see him for months straight he's so infatuated and preoccupied with having sex.

Solomon ***willfully*** fell into this situation with all these various women and it caused him to forsake all that God had bestowed upon him. Solomon took it all for granted, the bequeathed king who was specifically supposed to be a beacon of light leading God's people in a world of evil.

"He had seven hundred wives, princesses, and three hundred concubines, and his wives turned his heart away. For when Solomon was old, his wives turned his heart away after other gods; and his heart was not wholly devoted to the Lord his God, as the heart of David his father had been."

Solomon was handed a prophetic life on a silver platter and he temporarily traded it all for physical rewards in this life in the form of an orgy of sex. Solomon had 700 wives and 300 concubines. **That's a THOUSAND WOMEN** that were specifically reserved for King Solomon **alone** to have sex with. Do you think a king would share his women with men of lesser societal status? Absolutely not. He was fornicating with all these women as fast as he was able. This is a very significant thing to understand, as this is a very large number.

We just went over the initial women-sex part of the equation, but it says that Solomon's heart wasn't turned away until he was **old.** What is the whole point, the basis of the Great Plan? For man to be immortal so that getting 'old' won't be an issue.

In Solomon's day it certainly was an issue to him because he wanted to stay on Earth in his physical body and keep making love to all those beautiful women, who were probably the most attractive women around at the time. Good sex is certainly not worth going against God though. As he was growing older he was losing his good looks and **especially** his virility, they didn't have Viagra back then remember. His women wanted him physically and he was waning as he aged, so his wives coaxed him into the occult to try and turn not only his sex life around, but to try and prolong his life in general.

Who better to ask for more time in **this** world, this 3D existence, than Father Time himself, the god of time and god of this world, Satan.

> *"In the beginning was the ***Golden Age***, when men of their own accord, without threat of punishment, without laws, maintained good faith and did what was right. . . . The earth itself, without compulsion, untouched by the hoe, unfurrowed by any share, produced all things spontaneously. . . . It was a season of everlasting Spring.*

Rabbinical sources recount that men lived under very favorable conditions before the Deluge, and that these contributed to their sinfulness: They knew neither toil nor care and as a consequence of their extraordinary prosperity they grew insolent.

It appears to be generally accepted that Solomon, rather than David, introduced the six-pointed star (in legend at least), and that it also represents the Chaldean supreme deity Saturn. Since the Chaldean Saturn apparently equates to Chronos or Aion, a deity with a Father Time quality, Solomon's use of the hexagram may appear a bit less startling than many allege."

-Roman poet Ovid (43 BC – 17 AD) from his book 'Metamorphoses'

Solomon was virtually like an ancient movie or rock star and surely had thousands of women throwing themselves at him, hoping he would want them in particular. This would have built his ego up to the Moon and he would have certainly come under pressure on many fronts to retain his youthful vim and vigor.

He eventually realized that he made a huge mistake seeking Satan's help, ditched the Saturn worship and came crawling back to God. This is when he wrote Ecclesiastes. When you know what you are learning here, go back and read Ecclesiastes and it will make so much more sense, as 1 Enoch and many other works make so much more sense figuring everything in, everything we've gone over.

The part where it says **"....and his heart was not *wholly* devoted to the Lord his God, as the heart of David his father *had been*."**

This tells us exactly what happened. Solomon was worshipping both Satan and God at the same time with the twisted view of the true Satanists that Satan is just another facet, another part of God.

Remember, the position of Judaism today that they believe 'God is one'. This is the interpretation of the main message from the Torah stuffed into those black tefillin cubes. God makes both good and evil, and I don't disagree.

However, God **doesn't want us to take advantage/exploit this**. At least not the ones whose names were written in the Book of Life from the foundation of this world. This is for the ones of Satan to exploit in order to test humanity, not God's own people, the ancient Israelis.

Unfortunately, the ancient Israelites exploited the duality-thing and that it's an eternal law of balance, and Solomon, being as 'wise' as he was, moved to exploit this to the benefit of his physical body and the Nation of Israel as a whole.

It's no different today as it is back then. Certainly today not all Jews are part of this conspiracy just as back then, but some certainly are, the same as not all Christians or Freemasons are part of the Great Plan but Satanic elements contained in both are.

> *"For Solomon went after Ashtoreth the goddess of the Sidonians and after Milcom the detestable idol of the Ammonites. Solomon did what was evil in the sight of the Lord, and did not follow the Lord fully, as David his father had done."*

Knowing what we do, it is easy to establish that Ashtoreth equates to Astarte, Ishtar, Isis, and Semiramis. Also, Milcom equates to Molech/Baal/Osiris/Nimrod. What this is telling us is that Solomon introduced the Babylonian Mystery Religion to the Israelites as a way of ruling over them and gaining favors for himself and the Nation of Israel from Satan in the process. Satan would have been more than eager to reward these exact people for straying from the Most High.

"Then Solomon built a high place for Chemosh the detestable idol of Moab, on the mountain which is east of Jerusalem, and for Molech the detestable idol of the sons of Ammon. Thus also he did for all his foreign wives, who burned incense and sacrificed to their gods.

In the above quote, Chemosh equates to Saturn/Satan, and Molech equates to Nimrod. The term 'Molech' means 'king', who is a representation of an earthly ruler, the first king under Satan post-Flood, King Nimrod.

I'm going to use a verse from Judges to back up what I'm saying here with regards to the identity of Chemosh in particular:

Now Jephthah sent messengers to the king of the sons of Ammon, saying, "What is between you and me, that you have come to me to fight against my land?"

The king of the sons of Ammon said to the messengers of Jephthah, "Because Israel took away my land when they came up from Egypt, from the Arnon as far as the Jabbok and the Jordan; therefore, return them peaceably now."

But Jephthah sent messengers again to the king of the sons of Ammon, and they said to him, "Thus says Jephthah, 'Israel did not take away the land of Moab nor the land of the sons of Ammon. For when they came up from Egypt, and Israel went through the wilderness to the Red Sea and came to Kadesh, then Israel sent messengers to the king of Edom, saying, "Please let us pass through your land," but the king of Edom would not listen. And they also sent to the king of Moab, but he would not consent. So Israel remained at Kadesh. Then they went through the wilderness and around the land of Edom and the land of Moab, and came to the east side of the land of Moab, and they camped beyond the Arnon; but they did not enter the territory of Moab, for the Arnon was the border of Moab. And Israel sent messengers to Sihon *king of the Amorites, the king of Heshbon, and Israel said to him, "Please let us pass through your land to our place." But Sihon did not trust Israel to pass through his territory; so Sihon gathered all his people and camped in Jahaz and fought with Israel. The Lord, the God of Israel, gave Sihon and all his people into the hand of Israel, and they defeated them; so Israel possessed all the land of the Amorites, the inhabitants of that country. So they possessed all the territory of the Amorites, from the Arnon as far as the Jabbok, and from the wilderness as far as the Jordan. Since now the Lord, the God of Israel, drove out the Amorites from before His people Israel, are you then to possess it? *****Do you not possess what Chemosh your god gives you to possess?***** So whatever the Lord our God has driven out before us, we will possess it. Now are you any better than Balak the son of Zippor, king of Moab? Did he ever strive with Israel, or did he ever fight against them? While Israel lived in Heshbon and its villages, and in Aroer and its villages, and in all the cities that are on the banks of the Arnon, three hundred years, why did you not recover them within that time? I therefore have not sinned against you, but you are doing me wrong by making war against me; may the Lord, the Judge, judge today between the sons of Israel and the sons of Ammon."'*

But the king of the sons of Ammon disregarded the message which Jephthah sent him."

-Judges 11:12-28

In the above passage, the messenger is relaying to the king of the sons of Ammon this particular question from the message of the prophet Jephthah, **'Do you not possess what Chemosh your god gives you to possess?'**

Who is the only 'god' who has that kind of power besides the Most High God? That would be exactly Satan, the god of this world, also known as Saturn/Chemosh.

Here's the balance of the original passage from 1 Kings we're breaking down:

> *"Now the Lord was angry with Solomon because his heart was turned away from the Lord, the God of Israel, who had appeared to him twice, and had commanded him concerning this thing, that he should not go after other gods; but he did not observe what the Lord had commanded. So the Lord said to Solomon, "Because you have done this, and you have not kept My covenant and My statutes, which I have commanded you, I will surely tear the kingdom from you, and will give it to your servant. Nevertheless I will not do it in your days for the sake of your father David, but I will tear it out of the hand of your son. However, I will not tear away all the kingdom, but I will give one tribe to your son for the sake of My servant David and for the sake of Jerusalem which I have chosen."*

I don't know about you, but if God came to see me **in Person**, any inclination of disobeying His exact orders from that point until they put me in the ground would be reduced to nothing.

There is no greater reward in this life than to serve God. It's very simple: physical rewards are temporary, spiritual rewards are for eternity. Eternity is a long time, and compared to the 80+/-years we are here on Earth it is an incomprehensible number of years. We are just here for the blink of God's eye.

Solomon knew that evil is needed in this world by God and Solomon capitalized on that, but God doesn't approve of what Solomon did, not at all.

His sex drive got the best of him and his body, heart and mind turned against his soul. Our physical bodies are quite literally slaves of Satan. This has been man's downfall since we were put here in the Garden of Eden. We are slaves to our physical bodies that Satan has extreme power of influence over, because this is his world. We are made of physical components of ***his*** world, that in turn he has been made god over by the Most High God in order to test the interdimensional souls of those whose names are in the Book of Life.

> *"I know that everything God does will remain forever; there is nothing to add to it and there is nothing to take from it, for God has so worked that men should fear Him. That which is has been already and that which will be has already been, for God seeks what has passed by.*
>
> *Furthermore, I have seen under the sun that in the place of justice there is wickedness and in the place of righteousness there is wickedness. I said to myself, "God will judge both the righteous man and the wicked man," for a time for every [c] matter and for every deed is there. I said to myself concerning the sons of men, "God has surely tested them in order for them to see that they are but beasts." For the fate of the sons of men and the fate of beasts is the same. As one dies so dies the other; indeed, they all have the same breath and there is no advantage for man over beast, for all is vanity. All go to the same place. All came from the dust and all return to the dust."*
>
> *-Ecclesiastes 3:14-20, the words of King Solomon*

Satan is real and if you help him fulfill his mission then he has the capability to reward you with money and power in this life and that, in my opinion, is the honest truth. He will show you exactly what you need to do to get it. It's called participation in the 'The Great Plan' and you go from 'test-***ee***' to 'test-***er***' in the service of Satan.

Sir Isaac Newton's statement that for every action there is an equal but opposite reaction. This is a law of physics, which also helps to explain our reality and the duality the people running the world believe in and follow.

Does this quote from my first book make more sense now?:

"Yes, Lucifer is God, and unfortunately Adonay is also God. For the eternal law is that there is no light without shade, no beauty without ugliness, no white without black, for the absolute can only exist as two Gods: darkness being necessary to light to serve as its foil as the pedestal is necessary to the statue, and the brake to the locomotive...

...Thus, the doctrine of Satanism is a heresy; and the true and pure philosophic religion is the belief in Lucifer, the equal of Adonay; but Lucifer, God of Light and God of Good, is struggling for humanity against Adonay, the God of darkness and evil."

-Albert Pike, 33rd Degree Freemason, explaining the belief system of the people running the Great Plan

God continued to send prophets into His peoples' midst, however, telling them to repent and that's where so much of the Old Testament comes from: God reprimanding His people over Satan/Antichrist worship. They are a **'stubborn people'** remember (God's words, not mine).

The Saturn worship by Solomon is ***exactly*** how he became associated with the Seal of Solomon, which is exactly the star of Rephan from the Book of Amos. **Rephan *is* the god Saturn**, and Saturn as you should now know is exactly Satan.

The Bible, at least all the versions we have today, doesn't directly tell us what really happened with the story of Solomon, not saying directly that Solomon turned to Satan worship, but leaving it up to us to connect the dots today because **knowledge is indeed increasing**.

Backsliding, Israel Examples

"In those days I also saw that the Jews had married women from Ashdod, Ammon and Moab. As for their children, half spoke in the language of Ashdod, and none of them was able to speak the language of Judah, but the language of his own

people. So I contended with them and cursed them and struck some of them and pulled out their hair, and made them swear by God, "You shall not give your daughters to their sons, nor take of their daughters for your sons or for yourselves. Did not Solomon king of Israel sin regarding these things? Yet among the many nations there was no king like him, and he was loved by his God, and God made him king over all Israel; nevertheless the foreign women caused even him to sin."

-Nehemiah 13:23-26

There's one last item to attend to here that took me a little while to sort out, but I think I have understood it to the point I can explain it simply.

What we need to go over now actually challenged my faith at first learning this, but I researched and found resolve. I don't want to leave this pit open for you to stumble into if and when you start looking into Saturn worship and how it got spread around all over the ancient world with the BMR by the proponents of the Great Plan.

This has to do with the term 'El' or also 'el', either by itself or as a prefix or suffix. There is quite a mess about this term, because 'El' is exactly what the ancient Canaanites called Saturn/Satan, and the Hebrew language is based on the Canaanite language, which you probably didn't know and I didn't either until I was into my research on the term 'El'.

"Then the word of the Lord came to me, saying, "Son of man, make known to Jerusalem her abominations and say, 'Thus says the Lord God to Jerusalem, "Your origin and your birth are from the land of the Canaanite, your father was an Amorite and your mother a Hittite. As for your birth, on the day you were born your navel cord was not cut, nor were you washed with water for cleansing; you were not rubbed with salt or even wrapped in cloths. No eye looked with pity on

you to do any of these things for you, to have compassion on you. Rather you were thrown out into the open field, for you were abhorred on the day you were born."
-Ezekiel 16:1-5

If you look at the cover of this book, you will see I have displayed my middle name 'Michael' as 'Micah'el'. This was to make people question why I had done this, hoping they would investigate for themselves why the 'el' was made to stand alone. It's because God is in my name, and He is in many names used today. Michael. Daniel. Gabriel. Ezekiel. Joel. Etc. It seems God's angels all have 'el' in their names also, along with many Biblical prophets. Remember the ancient Hebrew name for Satan, Azaz-***el***? Azazel means 'strong one of God', or my own name Michael means 'who is like God'.

'El' as a god, and using 'El' for the god Saturn in particular, originated in ancient Canaan. The god 'El', referring to Saturn/ Satan, was the chief god of the Canaanites.

The ancient Israelites took this term for Saturn from the Canaanites, and this is the basis of their position that 'God is one', God made everything in existence, so the term 'el' came to also represent God to them because they knew of the universal law of duality. They started associating this two-letter term with God, but in different contexts 'el' means different things.

'El' by itself as a proper noun means specifically Saturn/Satan. 'el' lower case means God the composite of our Heavenly Father, both good and bad, or 'God is one' from the verses I listed already. The term 'El Elyon' is specifically meant to refer to God, and translates to 'God Most High'. In Genesis 14, Melchizedek is specified as a priest of the Most High God, or El Elyon. This is to specify our Heavenly Father as opposed to Saturn. This is also exactly why our Heavenly Father is called the Most High God, to differentiate between Him and the god of this world, Satan. There is more to it than this, but this is the gist of it to the best of my understanding.

"Then after his return from the defeat of Chedorlaomer and the kings who were with him, the king of Sodom went out to meet him at the valley of Shaveh (that is, the King's Valley). And Melchizedek king of Salem brought out bread and wine; now he was a priest of God Most High. He blessed him and said,

"Blessed be Abram of God Most High,
Possessor of heaven and earth;
And blessed be God Most High,
Who has delivered your enemies into your hand."
-Genesis 14:17-20, NASB

"And the Melech Sodom went out to meet him after his return from the defeat of Kedorlaomer, and of the melachim that were with him, at the Valley of Shaveh, which is the Valley of the King. And Malki-Tzedek Melech Shalem brought forth lechem and yayin and he was the kohen of El Elyon.

And he blessed him, and said, "Baruch Avram by El Elyon, Creator of Shomayim v'Aretz; And baruch El Elyon, Who hath delivered thine enemies into thy hand. And he gave him ma'aser (tithe) of all."
-Genesis 14:17-20, Orthodox Jewish Bible

The alternate to my interpretation and explanation is that Judaism is a pagan religion originally based on the Great Plan, and Jesus was just a fictional character who never existed, and that the Bible, both Old and New Testaments, are not the word of God and were created purely to control us using religion. Now, I don't believe any of that, but as I considered these possibilities while sorting this particular issue out it brought pressure to bear on my faith. I certainly do explore every avenue in my research, it is the only way.

All evidence, in my mind, points to the contrary of my 'alternate possibility' of our faith. I always think about and explore without hesitation all aspects, all facets, and all positions of everything I look into. I have to. As a truth-seeker you have to entertain all avenues, fearing no paths to get to the real truth.

That's all I ever wanted, the truth. If I had found the evidence to lose my faith this would be a completely different book, in fact you wouldn't even be reading it.

I didn't lose my faith, it's stronger than it's ever been in my life knowing what I know. Our god is God Most High and His Earthly Representation is our Messiah and God, Jesus Christ.

Now let's wrap this thing up. I've got to get working on that third book, friend.

Chapter 7

THE AWAKENING

"... if the sentinel sees the sword coming and does not blow the trumpet and the people are not warned, and a sword comes and takes a person from them, he is taken away in his iniquity; but his blood I will require from the sentinel's hand."
- Ezekiel 33:6, the words of God, JHV

Truly there is an awakening going on right now, and it's worldwide. People are waking up to the fact that something's not right. They are realizing that the way the world is going is not in their best interests, but in the interests of the people who perpetually run the show. The people whose eyes are beginning to open are going to want to know what's really going on, and we need to make our case against the forces of evil known....to let them know about the factual existence of the New World Order.

The proponents of the New World Order have done everything they can over the millennia to put up barriers between us and God as part of our test. Almost like a basic training course in the army. They set up a field of fences, barbed wire, water hazards and even land mines for us to step on trying to get to the real truth in order to test us.

My life as a former atheist, now a Sentinel of the Most High, is testament to this. I fell into the traps in the Satanic Matrix time and time again, until I woke up to the New World Order, researched it and 'passed my test', getting saved by Jesus. These books are my testament of the factual evidence as to why I'm now counted among the saved brethren.

Now that the contents of this book have been safely delivered, you can clearly see that we are, beyond any shadow of a doubt, staring down a truly Satanic conspiracy; there is no other way to put it.

"These things I have spoken to you, so that in Me you may have peace. In the world you have tribulation, but take courage; I have overcome the world."
-John 16:23

People know something is drastically wrong, it is our duty as Christians, as Americans, and as human beings to let them know what is really going on.

I need your help, friend. The hard part is researching and writing these books I'm creating to try and wake up humanity. The easy part is for you to pass on to others that I can show them the truth of our situation.

Many souls have been saved by people reading what I have to say, I have the emails and messages to factually back this up, and those are just the ones who took the time to track me down to let me know this. Dozens of people have contacted me one way or another, so the ones I didn't personally come into contact with could number in the hundreds or even thousands souls saved. We are certainly doing God's work by effecting this spiritual awakening around us through our knowledge of the New World Order and the sharing of it. Most people are smart enough to connect the dots once you show them, you just have to get their attention. Plant a seed and you never know what might happen.

Please let everyone you know of the existence of my books. Thank you.

"Who will stand up for Me against evildoers?
Who will take his stand for Me against those who do wickedness?"
-Psalms 94:16

Chapter 7/A

HIGHWAY TO HELL

"Living easy, living free, season ticket on a one way ride
Asking nothing, leave me be, taking everything in my stride
Don't need reason, don't need rhyme, ain't nothing that I'd rather do
Going down, party time, my friends are gonna be there too

I'm on the highway to Hell, on the highway to Hell
Highway to Hell, I'm on the highway to Hell

No stop signs, speed limits, nobody's gonna slow me down
Like a wheel, gonna spin it, nobody's gonna mess me around
Hey, Satan, paying my dues, playin' in a rockin' band
Hey, mamma, look at me, I'm on my way to the promised land

I'm on the highway to Hell"

-The song 'Highway to Hell' by AC/DC, 1979

"I live my life like there's no tomorrow, and all I've got I had to steal

Least I don't need to beg or borrow, yes, I'm living at a pace that kills

I'm Runnin' with the Devil....runnin' with the Devil.... runnin' with the Devil"

-The song 'Runnin' with the Devil' by Van Halen, 1978

"Burn out the day, burn out the night. I can't see no reason to put up a fight. I'm living for giving the devil his due......and I'm burning for you"

-The song 'Burnin' For You' by Blue Oyster Cult, 1981

Satan is coming out in the open, even being promoted as 'cool', as we're at the threshold of witnessing the conclusion to the 'Great Plan', full blown Satanic one world government with a resurrected King Nimrod helming it as the infamous Antichrist. The one world government is in place as you know, the United Nations, and when the United States falls the UN will rise to become the one, true global superpower.

Now, the term 'Antichrist' as it is used originally doesn't mean 'against Christ'....it means 'in the stead of' Christ, a substitution. He is an imposter, a counterfeit, a fake who will come back to Earth and claim that he is rightfully the 'Christ', the one whose symbols we wear, whose holidays we celebrate, and whose day the Christians worship on, Sunday.

And he'll be 100% correct......

There has been a concerted effort by the proponents of the New World Order since the end of World War II to turn our society and our world upside down. They've been doing this for thousands of years, but it's different this time as we factor advanced technology into the mix.

This 'death spiral' began in earnest in the 1950s with the merging of music and electricity and the introduction of something you may have heard of called 'Rock and Roll'.

Music has been a huge part of my life ever since I was born. My parents used to blast Led Zeppelin, Pink Floyd, and Grand Funk Railroad among others when I was a 3-year-old toddler in 1973, whipping me into a frenzy on my rocking horse that was positioned right in front of the speakers as I listened to the power chords and thumping bass drum pounding into my head. Little did they know that they were unintentionally planting the seeds of rebellion in me at that young, impressionable age.

The lyrics to the songs I listed above I listened to as a (still impressionable) 10-year-old boy around 1980, same speakers, same stereo, same radio station (KISW in Seattle), different time and location.

Now, you might be thinking to yourself that these are just harmless lyrics written by unassuming rock musicians with no agenda.....or are they?

> *"My true belief about Rock 'n' Roll--and there have been a lot of phrases attributed to me over the years--is this: I believe this kind of music is demonic. ... A lot of the beats in music today are taken from voodoo, from the voodoo drums. If you study music in rhythms, like I have, you'll see that is true. I believe that kind of music is driving people from Christ."*
>
> *-Little Richard, from 'The Life and Times of Little Richard', 1994*

> *"Rock has always been the Devil's music . . . I believe rock and roll is dangerous . . . I feel we're only heralding something even darker than ourselves."*
>
> *-David Bowie, Rolling Stone, Feb. 12, 1976*

The man who is called 'the father of rock and roll', Robert Johnson, was said to have made a deal with the Devil himself for guitar-playing prowess and I've seen enough evidence to believe this. Johnson was immortalized by Eric Clapton's song 'Crossroads' and the movie of the same name.

If you look into the backgrounds of the biggest names in music today, such as Katy Perry, Jay-Z, Rihanna, Lady Gaga, etc. all the way back through the decades of the popular music into the 1960s when the Tavistock Institute lit the fuse on the counterculture revolution still going on today, you will see they are littered with occultism and even outright Satanism.

Now, music is based on numbers, and more even more specific is that it is based in sacred geometry. You have set amounts of certain sounds, then it progresses to something else. If you don't follow a certain order the song will not sound good. I learned this well from being in a band myself and having to learn how to write lyrics for songs. Most songs are comprised of groups of even-numbers of notes, fours, sixes and eights typically. So a song might go 8 'body' lines, 4 'bridge' lines and then 4,6 or 8 lines of chorus. Then start that same formula over 2 or 3 more times and viola, you have a song.

There is something very special about music and how it effects the psyche of the human being, and the influence of music as a child no doubt led to me wanting to get involved with that realm as an adult. Most people don't know I was a lead singer in a heavy metal band in Seattle in the mid to late 1990s, wore all black leather and had long hair.

That energized feeling I got as a child from listening to hard rock I longed to create as I got old enough to do so, and I did.

I was hell on wheels in my teens and twenties and shouldn't be alive today to tell you the truth. My appetite for sex, drugs and rock n' roll should have done me in. Was it because of demonic influence as a young child through the popular music of the day?

Satan showed up in force in the late 1970s in music, and when I was 10 years old I was having these lyrics glorifying exactly Satan inserted into my head daily.

How about another song from Blue Oyster Cult called **'Don't Fear the Reaper'**. The (Grim) Reaper is the same thing as that character called 'Death', the same as Kronos...Saturn...Satan.

Here is a close-up of a symbol displayed on the cover of the album that contains the song, 'Don't Fear the Reaper', called 'Agents of Fortune'. This is also the official symbol of the band Blue Oyster Cult. Please note the finger pointing directly at the symbol:

Does this look familiar to you at all? It should, it's a stylized astrological symbol of Saturn, the cross and sickle.

This symbol can be found on every album of Blue Oyster Cult. Whoever was pulling the strings of this band was obviously an occultist/Satanist. Most people don't even know what a 'blue oyster' is. Well, let me tell you that a 'blue oyster' is sex-slang from the New York City gay scene of the 60s and 70s, and equates to the blood-engorged head of a man's penis during prolonged sexual excitement without coming to orgasm and taking on a bluish-color.

As you know, sodomy and especially male-on-male sodomy is promoted heavily by Satan himself to corrupt our society in God's eyes. New York-based Blue Oyster Cult was up to their eyeballs in Satanic influence, penning the songs that I was raised on as a child among many others heavily influenced by Satan. Lots of perversion hidden right in front of our faces. Most people don't know that 1970s hitmakers 'Steely Dan' were named after a sex toy......

The above image is part of the entire album cover, showing a magician holding four Tarot cards. The version of these in particular are **Aleister Crowley's 'Thoth Tarot'** cards. The cards are Death (Satan), the King (Nimrod/Antichrist), the Queen (Semiramis/Astarte/Isis/etc.), and the Sun (Tammuz/Nimrod reborn). So you have within these four cards a tribute to both Saturn worship and the Babylonian Mystery Religion.

What is the biggest Saturday Night Live skit of recent years? The 'More Cowbell' skit with Christopher Walken and Will Ferrell. And what song was it that they had to play over and over?

Blue Oyster Cult's 'Don't Fear the Reaper'..........

Now, virtually all the 'best' music from the 1960s onward was created under the influence of hardcore drugs like cocaine, meth, heroin, etc. This is because these extreme human-psyche manipulators open up your physical being, even your soul, to demonic/Satanic influence.

This goes from the Beach Boys and the Beatles in the 60s, Led Zeppelin and Fleetwood Mac in the 70s, Metallica to Guns n' Roses in the 80s, Nirvana and Alice in Chains in the 90s, and all the way to today. All of these people were documented to have been on heroin, cocaine, etc. during the writing of the vast majority of their music, at least their hit songs. This is because of the demonic influence that comes upon your being while on these drugs. I used to do these drugs and I can testify to knowing what it feels like to be on those drugs and the best word I could use to describe being high on cocaine or meth is 'demonic'.

There are, however, some good things to come out of the modern music industry and I'll leave you with this on the topic of music: The story of singer Dan Peek of the band 'America'.

America is a long-time favorite band of mine, many hit songs I'm sure you've heard at one point or another if you're in your 30s or older, and when I found this out through my research it brought me to tears of joy.

At America's zenith in 1977, a drugged-out Dan Peek walked away from his band and left modern-day Babylon behind to walk into the arms of our Lord and Savior Jesus Christ. He left it all behind. The drugs. The money. The decadence. Right after he left the band his million-dollar mansion burned to the ground in a forest fire in California and he went broke soon after. He lost it all but gained something even better, salvation. He traded his life on Earth for a new one working for God, with no regrets, to the day he died in 2011.

Music is not the only entertainment industry Satan has been promoted in lately. If you look it up, a character named Azazel turned up recently in one of the X-men movies and he looked exactly like the general public would expect the real Satan/Azazel to look like. He had red skin, goatee, dressed in sinister all-black (color of Saturn) **with a pointed devil's tail no less.**

If you look it up, Azazel's character description by Marvel Comics seems to suggest he is exactly Satan, even promoting it.

Azazel in the X-men is only one of hundreds and even thousands of Satanic 'appearances' in modern times, keeping in mind stuff like the symbol of Blue Oyster Cult from the previous image. Hopefully you are aware of the plethora of 'Illuminati' symbolism that permeates both adult and children's film and television programming, with Disney being arguably the kingpin of this realm. Remember from my first book, the '33 Club' at Disneyland in California? Of course you do.

We are under constant media assault by the proponents of the New World Order and the temptations available to mankind to test us is off the chart these days. Between rebellious/tantric music to online pornography to designer drugs to online cheating websites, we are truly living in the modern day Babylon, exactly as planned, exactly as prophesized.

I intend on writing one of the installments of my book series about music, the industry, and the artists and how intricately intertwined with Satan and the supernatural music really is.

Hopefully we're around long enough for me to write it and you to read it, friend.

Chapter 7/B

ORDER OUT OF CHAOS

"We are on the verge of a global transformation. All we need is the right major crisis and the nations will accept the New World Order."

—David Rockefeller

I'm just going to very briefly comment on the current state of affairs as they are, dated May of 2016, the re-release of this newly remodeled second book of mine.

Well, here in the United States it seems everyone is at everyone else's throats. The Mainstream Media has whipped up everyone's emotions to polarize and divide us against each other like never before. Black vs. White. Men vs. Women. Capitalists vs. Socialists. Legal citizens vs. illegal aliens. Republican vs. Democrat. LGBT community vs. 'straights'. Muslims vs. Jews/Christians, Rich vs. poor. Etc.

It seems 'electing' a black President would have moved race relations forward but with this Satanic-puppet Obama they have gone backwards by 50 years and now there's a powder keg of angst waiting to go off....and it will.

Now, we have possibly the first woman President on deck, Hillary Clinton. Are you kidding me? Hillary is a career criminal and a full-on Establishment/NWO puppet and this is the best, most moral and qualified woman in the United States to be the first woman President? This is an absolute disgrace but no surprise given the state of things these days. People just don't care, we're that far gone.

The proponents of the New World Order know we don't care so they are fully moving their agenda forward at high speed now on many fronts.

At the spear point of their attack on Christianity in particular and moral society in general is the shoving of the 'gay agenda' down our throats. If you don't approve of men having sex with other men then that makes you a hateful, bigoted person.... according to ***them.*** Isn't that the only real difference between gays and straights? One group's differentiation revolves around their deviant sexual desires and that's about it. This is mainly a gay, male issue being driven by militant, demon-possessed males with the sodomite-Illuminati males as the puppet masters of all of this. Male-on-male sodomy originated as a Satanic-ceremony-act, and everything in honor of Satan, the god of this world, is being pushed these days.

I'm not anti-gay either, I fully follow the commandment of Jesus to treat others like I want them to treat me. I'm just stating my position on the 'gay agenda' according to what I know. My favorite uncle was gay, lived that lifestyle and got taken out by the first wave of AIDS cases in the 1980s. The gays will stand before God someday as I will to account for their actions, so I don't condemn them for succumbing to demonic interference which is where homosexuality is rooted in my opinion.

It is factually documented with studies that gay men have an average of **hundreds if not thousands** of sex partners in their lives. The average heterosexual male barely makes it into double-digits on average, so you can't tell me that the gay agenda doesn't revolve around a deviant sexual lifestyle and wanting to bring more into the mix through confusion and coercion.

The radical gay agenda has already eviscerated the sanctity of marriage between a man and a woman and as of 2016 our entire sexual identities are under attack as they seek to allow men and women to use each other's restrooms respectively. Complete chaos as we speak, all by plan.

The flames of religious tension are beginning to burn, being fanned on one side, and the other side...a deception is unfolding. The Syrian refugee crisis which is flooding Europe with hundreds of thousands of Muslims is an event planned many years ago by the Illuminati. By introducing Muslims, who have no intention of assimilating with Christians or European society in general and actually the opposite=they want to convert the Christians to Islam. This will begin to create the tension and accompanying problems that the Antichrist will solve someday, looking like the 'savior' he really isn't. This is why on the other side of the equation the Pope and the Vatican are pushing an interfaith agenda, with the Pope even going so far as to say recently that the Koran is as valid as the Bible and that Islam and Christianity worship the same 'god'.

Not only do we have a manufactured refugee issue, World War III is on deck as I type this. If the powder keg goes off in Syria you better believe there will be a draft and if you are a male, aged 18-25 you can expect to be shipped off to fight in the latest Illuminati-manufactured war and don't expect to come back either with what is coming. Heck, with all the feminazisism and gender-bending going on these days they just might draft women too and send them into the meat grinder to die with the men...just saying.

Onward to illegal immigration. Here in the United States, the Mainstream Media is portraying the illegal immigrant issue as a race issue, pitting white United States citizens against illegal Mexicans. This is not a racial issue at all as I went over in my first book. **Mexicans are a nationality, not a race.** Mexico itself has a massive wall between them and Guatemala to **THEIR** southern border. Mexico has stringent rules about illegals in their country and don't give them a dime in benefits, but we're the bad guys because we oppose illegal immigration????

If Mexicans were 'white', I and everyone else with half a brain would still be just as opposed to members of a third world country invading ours, disregarding our laws, jumping the border and then jumping on the financial backs of hard-working, tax-paying citizens of the United States and bleeding our already-ailing social service systems dry. Illuminati minions like George Soros have been documented to be funding not only the illegal alien marches and propaganda but also paying out of his deep Illuminati coffers to fan black-white racial tensions with paid protesters. So much going on it's hard to keep up with all the chaos the NWO is unleashing right now upon the citizens of the United States.

It is a certainty that those long lines of 'clouds' that appear some days and magically not the next, the 'chemtrails', are being sprayed for geoengineering, implementing HAARP along with them to create weather anomalies. HAARP is so important to understand I can't understate this fact. Please look into what they are capable of with this both fantastic and horrific technology. In the right hands we would be thriving now, what Nikola Tesla had intended, but in the wrong hands.... we have what we have today. Today the Satanists have the power to cause earthquakes, floods, tidal waves, heat waves, hurricanes, and even be able to implant voices into the heads of a targeted geographical area using this technology, it is that powerful.

So while all this craziness is going on, the globalists are trying to sneak the Trans-Pacific Partnership (TPP) past everyone. The TPP is a new, globalist trade agreement that should finish off our economy if passed. It is close to being signed off in 2016-2017 by our traitorous bought-and-paid members of Congress so please keep an eye on this.

Financial chaos is coming soon again like 2008, but when this one hits it will be the big one. The international bankers used up all their ammo pulling us out of the crash in 2008 and have nothing left but hyperinflation to stop a collapse again. When the dollar dies so does our country. This is the event that will trigger marital law. That is, if one of the other scenarios I just summarized doesn't come to pass first. Any one of these events could spiral out of control and they are not only likely to happen but to happen all at once, overwhelming the entire world.

> *"...that is, the one whose coming (Nimrod/Antichrist) is in accord with the activity of Satan with all power and signs and false wonders, and with all the deception of wickedness for those who perish, because they did not receive the love of the TRUTH so as to be saved."*
>
> *- 2 Thessalonians 2:9-10*

Chapter 7/C

SENTINELS OF GOD

"For thus hath the Lord said unto me, Go, set a sentinel, let him declare what he seeth."

-Isaiah 21:6

You should not be afraid to speak up about anything we are talking about in my works as long as we are sticking to truth and facts, which is what I aim to give you. You know that my works should be viewed as my opinion only until you verify for yourself everything I'm talking about.

On that note, it is important for you to know that everything I say, everything you say, everything others say on the internet whether it is typed words, audio and/or video, all is gathered up by the NSA and goes into your file. Even if you are not someone awake to the NWO and researching it and talking about it, you have a file. Everyone does. Every phone call. Every text. Every email. Every website you've been to, liked or commented on. Every financial transaction. Anything and everything you do that is electronic goes into your file, and it's filtered as it goes in looking for keywords to indicate you might be a trouble-maker. If you have a Social Security Number, you better believe you have a file with you SSN# right on it.....and a ranking. I'm sure I have a very high rank due to the amount of research I do into everything they want to keep secret, but I'm not intimidated by that. Not at all. All I'm after is the truth and even more so, the supernatural and eternal truths you get by plugging in all the physical truths in our world.

If anything, I would hope and pray that the agents assigned to my 'file' are looking into exactly what I and others are talking about, reading my books, following up to see that what I speak is not only the truth but that their families also will be impacted for the worse for what is coming if we don't head it off.

So with all this said, as long as you are speaking truth and not calling for violence you should have nothing to worry about, and you need to learn as much as you can about all this stuff so if and when the grid goes down you will be knowledgeable about what is really happening to pass on to those that don't.

So here's what I've been up to since releasing my first book, my plan of action in motion:

Right after I released my first book I headed right for YouTube, Facebook, and even Craigslist to start spreading word of my first book. I met like-minded people and began networking with them to spread word that I was offering my new book for free on PDF file at my website, samaritansentinel.com. If I was going to start a mass awakening of humanity with this book I put together I needed help. Lots of help. I was also selling it on Amazon, but the main push was to wake people up to the New World Order so I could try to stop it, or at least slow it down in order for my kids to have a better future because of....well, you know, the whole Satanic One World Government-deal.

I know that the bad stuff going on in the world and to come is supposed to happen, and that one day Jesus will come back and set things right, but I'm not one to sit on my hands idly as my family, friends, country, and faith are under attack by the forces of evil. I'm going to unsheathe my sword and fight to defend what I love and live for.

The best way to jump in swinging and get people on my side in force and in a hurry was to give my first book away for free and encourage others to pass it on down the line in emails as a PDF file to their friends and family to warn them about the existence of the New World Order.

I ran into a bunch of cool people on Facebook and they helped me tremendously to get the word out. I know that Facebook is largely a data-mining operation but as long as you aren't on there fomenting a violent revolution you don't have anything to worry about. We're just sticking to the facts and trying to network with others who would rather live knowing the truth than the lies we've been fed for thousands of years.

I met one guy in particular on Facebook in June of 2015 right after I had released the first version of the book you are holding now, and this guy was Eric Wilkinson. It appeared he was some sort of radio host, going by the name 'Spitfire the Freedom Fighter', so I threw it out there to come on his show to talk about my books. I ended up sending him a paperback copy of my first book. I think we kind of lost track of each other for a couple weeks after I sent him my first book and when we reconnected he said he had found Jesus after absorbing what I had to say in that book. This is not an uncommon occurrence you now know....just like I got saved researching and writing it.

So it went immediately from me coming on to do a single show with him to me turning into his sidekick for a new show called 'Spitfire and the Sentinel'. Eric is obviously 'Spitfire' and I was the 'Sentinel'.

A couple of months went by and we started having a live panel on our show of other people who were awake and wanted to talk about what they knew about the New World Order.

This one show we had done, Eric arranged a surprise for me: He had brought on the panel for the show a guy **HE** had a show with before he met me, and who he had had a falling out with but was patching things up. That guy was Mike Serour.

So as that particular show started I focused in on the hat Mike was wearing that night and it appeared there was a pentagram on it! So I asked him, **'What's up with that hat?'** I don't remember what his answer was exactly, but I came to find out he was a practicing LaVey Satanist. That's not the blood-drinking, baby-killing Satanists that run the world though. LaVey Satanism is glorified atheism-hedonism, so that gave me a little relief.

I ended up sending Mike a paperback of my first book and lo and behold......a few weeks after that.......**he got saved.**

HalleluYAH!!!!!!!

Spitfire pitched bringing Mike on the show with us permanently, and I agreed. We changed the name of the show to 'Spitfire and the Sentinels' (plural) and Mike was in. Soon after we added other 'Sentinels' to the show including Laurie Alexander, and a few other regulars. Mike has since started his own show, as has Laurie, but they still both appear with Spitfire and myself often.

So, to wrap this up, thank you so much for supporting me, for spreading the word of my works, and for standing up for the truth. Not everyone is brave enough to do this, but if we don't no one will. Don't be afraid to speak up. Ever.

I'm working on the third book as you read this, and I'm so glad to be working on it as it will be a book about God and Jesus, and the what, where and why I believe like I do that we're all part of His Divine Plan in this world.

To the extent that you believe in God, He will believe in YOU. My life and my works for Him are a testament and dedication to exactly this.

Keep your faith on high my friend, always remembering the Ten Commandments of God, and the Two Commandments of Jesus, always in His service, always for His honor and glory.

God bless you and yours. Thanks for being a fearless truth-seeker.

Until we talk again my friend,

-Sentinel Jeff Hays

Multi-Media

Please visit my associated media sites for more information about this book and the author. Please like my sites, send me friend requests, etc.:

Website: samaritansentinel.com
YouTube: Samaritan Sentinel
YouTube: Spitfire Sentinel
(I co-host a radio show on this channel)
G+: Samaritan Sentinel
Facebook: Samaritan Sentinel
Twitter:@sammysentinel
(Direct feed from FB Samaritan Sentinel page)

I am now live-in-person on YouTube to not only talk about the New World Order and to help spread word of my current and forthcoming works, but to give commentary on major current events as they unfold. I appear weekly along with Eric 'Spitfire' Wilkinson, Mike Serour, Laurie Alexander and many other highly-talented and awesome Sentinels of Truth who have banded together to create the best truth and information network on the internet. Please join us for breaking news and commentary like you will hear nowhere else in the mainstream or alternative media.

Here are our associated channels on YouTube, and there are more being added as we move forward:

Samaritan Sentinel
Spitfire Sentinel
Eric Spitfire

Mike Serour
The Underground Resistance Network
Linx To Truth
Damion Maynard
Revolution News And Information

Before alternative media reporter Pete Santilli was arrested in Oregon recently he was promoting our new show, Spitfire and the Sentinels, and I've known this man for 3 years now. He is a friend of mine and currently a political prisoner. Please visit his website thepetesantillishow.com to find information on how to write to him in jail (please do!), his current situation, and how to support him and Deb Jordan, his co-host. If you write him, make sure to tell him 'Sentinel Jeff Hays' sent you and he'll get a good laugh. Thanks for thinking of him.

Thanks

Thanks to Jesus for showing me so much truth to pass on to others. He kept me from harm for many years and finally called me into service. Thank You for saving me, I'm forever in Your service, a sentinel.

I'm just so grateful to know the people I know and to have met the people I have on this crazy journey, and I'm just thankful for all that they've done for me on my behalf. Thanks to you, friend, and all the other people who have taken the time to read what I have to say about what's going on in our world.

Thanks to my wife and kids for putting up with me needing to do what I was called to do, when I needed to do it. Many late nights and weekends I sat in my office working on these books and you've waited for me. I did it for God, but I did it for you too. Thank you. Love you.

Thanks Dad. Not anyone else than you would I would have wanted for a Dad. You instilled in me how to be a good human being and especially to speak up when someone is doing you or someone else wrong. That was certainly instrumental in motivating me to write these books to speak up and stand against the evil being factually perpetrated against us. Thanks for being there whenever I needed you. Love you.

Thanks to my brother Joel. You're my best friend too and that's pretty cool. Thanks bro. Love you.

Thanks to my step-sister Kendra. We've been through a lot over the years and you're still standing right with me and Joel. Thank you. Love you.

Thanks Artski, Nate, Jason V., Shawn B., Leonard W., Nantan P., Pete H. You're the best friends any guy could ask for. Thanks for being there for me. Love you all like brothers.

Thanks to my friend James, who I met a few months after I 'woke up' but before I got saved. When you told me the New World Order was all Satanic I thought you were wrong, but you were exactly right. Thanks for opening the door to help me to see the light. Hope you're well. Love you.

Thanks to my new friends and radio co-hosts: Eric 'Spitfire' Wilkinson, Mike Serour, Laurie Alexander, Bilal Talon, Linx Sivad, Damion Maynard, and more to come.

Thanks to my new friends and panel members on the various YouTube shows I appear on: Robbie Dee, Scott Schaller, Roberto Garza, Professor Doom, Jeff Lehman, Karen DeMayo, and more to come.

Thanks to the chat room people who follow our shows and back us up: Alaska bob, Alex Miller, Anne and David Post, Antfarmer, Athrenis i, Ash, Becky McCloskey-Dean, Blood Raw Truth, Brenda Gibson, Bsotf bsotf,Christopherallendunk, Clovis, Cubby70, Dallas Ahrens, Danyel Brown, Debbi Eddy, Deciduous Falling, Diane Pope, Dixie Barfield, Douglas Krantz, Doug Stanley, Eric Klemm, Girl Friday,Humberto Perez, I AM, J Grady, James D, Jeremy Roberts, Jeremy Voissem, Jimmy Cox, Johnny Cage, Jon Lennon, Justin Floyd, Karen Phillips, Kim Arnott, Kimberly LaChat, Kristen Cooper-Kucharik, Kristi Breit, Leanne Brown, Linda Lemmons, LM Barker, Lo K, Mary Brown, Michelle G, Nancybinthe313 xoxo, Pat Armstrong, Pete Zahutt, Proud American, Robert Gile, Robin, Sherrie LM, SRPiney, Tattoo, Teresa and Kenny Nunn, Terry Harris,Terry Lee, Toasted,Tom Guns, Travis, Weetreebonsai, Valley Forge Network, Zionik Ministries, and more to come.

Thanks to Sean Caron and his show 'Awakening Liberty' and Michael Howell and his show 'Fighting the Tyranny' for having me on and promoting my works.

Thanks to all my family and friends who I don't see often enough, you know who you are and I love you all dearly. Hopefully you are reading these words right this second and are awake to what's really going on in our world, and are making preparations for troubling times to come.

The cover illustration for this book and the first were designed by my friend David Dees. He is hands down the most influential and important political artist in the world. I see his art everywhere when I'm doing research and I really admired his work immediately after I woke up to the NWO. He's even a hero of mine because he's fearless in standing up for what he believes in. He has a book himself of some of his best political artwork in a 'coffee table' book and I highly recommend you get one to support him. This is a good book to leave out to be a conversation starter about the New World Order. He gives away the vast majority of his art for free to try and wake up humanity to the New World Order, so I regularly donate twenty bucks here and there to help him out. He appreciates any help you can give him my friends. He's also available to hire for art projects, including book covers. His website is ddees.com. Thanks for all your help, David. Love you man.

Thanks to my friend Charles Wahlheim. I'm so glad our paths crossed. I really enjoy our phone conversations about all the crazy things going on in our world and how they tie in to our faith. I can feel the strength of your faith in your voice and words, you're truly a representative of Jesus, always in His service. I loved your book *"The Truth, Claiming Your Birthright To Health: A Life Changing Perspective"* , now I just need to follow through and implement your plan of action....I'm working on it! Thanks for your input on this new book my friend. Love you like a brother.

Thanks to my friends who read the 'very'-rough draft of the first version of this book, I sure appreciated your input. I hope to meet every single one of you and thank you in person someday. Charles Wahlheim. Carlos Garcia. Curt Linderman. Jon Black. Maxine Lentz-Lausen. Josh Lawrence. Sharon Hundley Chesley.

Wild J. Mywildersyde. Angie Embry. John Callahan. Greg Filman. Brenda Herring.

Thanks to 'YouTube' Mike for reading my first book and putting it on YouTube. The video presentations you are making certainly back up everything I said in that first book. Hopefully you will sign up for this second book also my friend, all in His service. Again, to all, search for 'culling of man' on YouTube to find Mike's vids. I really enjoy them myself and look forward to every one of them.

If I forgot anyone, I certainly didn't mean to. God bless all my friends and family. God bless everyone, we're going to need it.

Thank you. Love you all like the brethren we truly are.

-Sentinel Jeff Hays

Bibliography

Although a large portion of the contents of this book was gleaned from the internet using Google, which was in turn used to access thousands of books and websites online, the following books were also influential in the composition of this book, coming into my physical possession during my time researching and writing this book:

Bevere, John *"The Bait of Satan"*
Box, G.H. and Dr. Moses Gaster *"The Apocalypse of Abraham"*
Bubeck, Mark I. *"The Adversary"*
Budge, E.A. Wallis *"The Gods of the Egyptians"*
Butler, Alan and Stephen Dafoe *"The Knights Templar Revealed"*
Cavendish, Richard *"Mythology"*
Charles, R.H. *"The Book of Enoch"*
Charles, R.H. *"The Book of Jubilees"*
Dickason, C. Fred *"Demon Possession & the Christian"*
Donnelly, Ignatius *"Atlantis: The Antediluvian World "*
Gitt, Werner *"Did God Use Evolution?"*
Glynn, Patrick *"God: The Evidence"*
Gray, John *"Near Eastern Mythology"*
Gygax, Gary *"Deities and Demigods"*
Hammer, David *"The Three Books of Enoch"*
Jeremiah, Dr. David *"What the Bible Says about Angels"*
John of the Gentiles, *"The False Prophet Azazel"*
Johnson, Ken *"Ancient Paganism"*
Johnson, Ken *"Ancient Seder Olam"*
Johnson, Ken *"The Ancient Book of Jasher"*
Kirban, Salem *"Satan's Mark Exposed"*

Kuntz, J. Kenneth *"The People of Ancient Israel"*
LaVey, Anton Szandor *"The Satanic Bible"*
Lindsey, Hal *"Satan is Alive and Well on Planet Earth"*
Long, Jeffrey *"Evidence of the Afterlife"*
Lubicz, R.A. Schwaller de *"Esotericism & Symbol"*
Lumpkin, Joseph B. *"The First and Second Books of Adam & Eve: The Conflict With Satan"*
Morgan, Giles *"Freemasonry"*
Orlov, Andrei A. *"Dark Mirrors"*
Perry, Marvin, Myrna Chase, James R. Jacob, Margaret C. Jacob, and Theodore H. Von Laue *"Western Civilization: Ideas, Politics & Society/Third Edition"*
Reader's Digest *"The World's Last Mysteries"*
Roebuck, Carl *"The World of Ancient Times"*
Shanks, Herschel *"Understanding the Dead Sea Scrolls"*
Visotzky, Burton L. and David E. Fishman *"From Mesopotamia to Modernity"*
Wahlheim, Charles *"The Truth, Claiming Your Birthright To Health: A Life Changing Perspective"*
Wilmshurst, W.L. *"The Meaning of Masonry"*
Woodrow, Ralph Edward *"Babylonian Mystery Religion"*

Printed in the USA
CPSIA information can be obtained
at www.ICGtesting.com
LVHW022147050124
768171LV00048B/953